AMO, AMAS, AMAT...

AND ALL THAT

AMO, AMAS, AMAT...

AND ALL THAT

How to become a Latin lover

Harry Mount

✳ **SHORT BOOKS**

First published in 2006 by
Short Books
3A Exmouth House
Pine Street, London EC1R OJH

10 9 8

A CIP catalogue record for this book
is available from the British Library.
ISBN 1-904977-54-5
(978-1-904977-54-4)
Printed in Great Britain by William Clowes Ltd, Beccles, Suffolk

For William and Mary

Mons Maximus et Mons Maxima

The study of the Classics teaches us to believe that there is something really great and excellent in the world, surviving all the shocks of accident and fluctuations of opinion, and raises us above that low and servile fear which bows only to present power and upstart authority.

William Hazlitt, *The Round Table* (1817)

Classics – from the Latin "*classicus, -a, -um*", meaning "of the highest class".

The New Oxford Dictionary of English (2001)

INTRODUCTION

David Beckham did not study Latin at Chingford School in Essex. The subject had long been off the state school curriculum by the time he got there in the late 1980s. Still, when it comes to his body art, the footballer is a dedicated Latinist. Of the nine tattoos on his body, three are in Latin (and two of the others, "Victoria" and "Romeo", are Latin-inspired names).

On his left forearm, he has the tricky little expression, "*Ut Amem et Foveam*" – "That I might love and cherish" – which makes careful and correct use of the subjunctive.

On his right forearm, he has the number of the football shirt he wears – 7 – although he opts for the Roman numeral, VII. Under the VII, Beckham has had his Manchester tattooist, Louis Malloy, retained since the footballer's days at Manchester United, write "*Perfectio in Spiritu*" – "Perfection in Spirit".

When it comes to his body art,
David Beckham is a dedicated Latinist

As I write, another sighting of a Latin celebrity tattoo has been made. On January 25th, 2006, the actress Angelina Jolie was seen passing through Heathrow Airport on the way to the economic summit at Davos, sporting a Latin tattoo on the lower slopes of her pregnant belly: "*Quod me nutrit me destruit*" – "What nourishes me destroys me."

As Miss Jolie is no doubt aware, the Latin on her tummy has echoes resonating back through the ages and through the pens of the greatest writers of all time. That's why she has the quote in Latin, and not in English or Swahili; for the same reason, she had it printed in a Gothic font – to give an impression of ancient wisdom.

The same desire for something old and high-brow means that Jacques Chirac wants to call his new European internet search-engine (if it comes off) "*Quaero*" – meaning "I seek" in Latin – rather than "*Je cherche*". And that's why Beckham, who has no formal knowledge of the language, turns to Latin for the skin-based words and numbers that he, his wife and several Madrid-based PR girls have to stare at day and, more often, night.

The big reason is the poshness of Latin. Because classics had no practical use, it tended to gain cachet among those who could afford to dedicate their time to fine prose, poetry and history rather than money-making disciplines such as science or engineering. It flourished in Britain's public schools – and today proper teaching of it only really survives there and in grammar schools.

And, though Beckham may not be aware of the history of Latin in the British education system, he will be aware of the inherited baggage of poshness that comes with the language.

He'll have noticed it in the mottos of football clubs (Arsenal's is *Victoria Concordia Crescit* – not "Posh Spice goes by Concorde", but "Victory grows through Togetherness"). He might have noticed the classical influence behind the grouped Ionic columns that frame the pedimented porch of his mock-Queen Anne house, Beckingham Palace in Sawbridgeworth, Hertfordshire. He may have seen Latin, too, in dates on war memorials and in epitaphs on tombstones, and carved as inscriptions on the facades of ancient houses. Wherever

Beckham has seen Latin, its setting will have been grand, or attached to the portentous things in life: birth, death, scholarship boards. The setting will also have tended to be an old one, or one that wants to conjure up connotations of oldness.

The knowledge that Latin has survived in written, if not in spoken, form for 2,500 years gives "*Ut ameam et foveam*" an elemental force that just isn't there in "That I might love and cherish". And this is the accumulated power of the language. Beckham may not be able to read Latin, but he will recognise it when he hears it in everyday speech: RIP (*requiescat in pace);* i.e (*id est*, "that is"); per se (a favourite with footballers – "I'm not moving to Real Madrid for the money per se") and so on.

All of these terms are mental triggers, little tics – dotted through the English language and cropping up in solid form all over England – which give Latin what the Manchester United marketing director would call tremendous branding potential.

And so to the point of this book: to make the jump from a Manchester tattooist's knowledge of Latin to a level where you can understand most of those inscriptions on tombstones, and get real pleasure from reading bits of Horace and Catullus, is not difficult.

If you never learned Latin at school – no matter. If you did, all the better. You might think you've forgotten it. You haven't. If you spent even the tiniest part of your teenage years learning dreary declensions and conjugations, the effort made to do so, and the young age at which you did it, means that a ghost of that knowledge is still there, tattooed to the back of your brain. Somewhere in your mind there still beat the old rhythms – *amo, amas, amat*; ablative absolutes; the future perfect; subjunctives.

As you go down the list, and the rules behind each idiom get a little more complicated, they may grow a little more faded, but all those rules need is a little memory boost, and they come flooding back. It will only take a quick trawl through this friendly Latin primer, with its reminders of a few of those declensions and conjugations, to bring the ghost to life. The joy that a little learning of Latin brings is immense.

Alexander Pope was quite wrong, by the way, when he said, "A little learning is a dangerous thing, drink deep or taste not the Pierian spring."

His miscalculation is particularly disappointing in somebody who certainly knew his classics, and would have known that Pieria was the place where, according to Hesiod, the Nine Muses were born – Clio, in charge of history; Urania, astronomy; Calliope, epic poetry; Melpomene, tragedies; Euterpe, harmony; Erato, lyric and love poetry; Terpsichore, dancing; Thalia, comedy; and Polyhymnia, music. All of these Muses are delightful subjects, of which a little knowledge can bring vast pleasure.

Okay, I do have to admit the Muses were Greek, like an awful lot of things absorbed by the Romans: tragedy, comedy, architecture; so many things in fact that Quintilian said with some relief, "*Satura quidem tota nostra est*" – "At least satire is completely ours."

But leave the Greek influences on Rome up to me. Wherever they are essential to our understanding, I will tie them in.

Satire: Peter Cook owed it all to Quintilian and the Romans

As for the power and beauty of Latin, this is perhaps best caught in the story of an English botanist on holiday in Rome a few springs ago. On a tour of the Colosseum (*colosseus, -a, - um* – colossal), the botanist saw a flower he'd never seen in Rome before. Puzzled, he started to look closely at the other flowers growing out of the flagstones of the old arena (from *harena, -ae, f.* – sand; i.e. the sand that was sprinkled in front of the *auditorium, -i, n.* – "a place of audience") and the cracks in the stone seats of the terraces. The flowers weren't native to Rome, or even to Italy. The bemused botanist left the Colosseum to go and look at the patches of grass nearby – under the Arch of Titus, over the Capitoline Hill, and in the stadium (*stadium, -i, n.* – a running track). He couldn't find a trace of these exotic flowers outside the arena at all.

When he took the flowers back to his Cambridge laboratory, he found that they had come from precise, verifiable places: Libya and Tunisia mostly. The only feasible explanation he could come up with was that the flowers had grown from seeds that had lodged in the coats of lions brought from Africa to eat Roman prisoners in the Colosseum 2000 years ago. The seeds must have fallen off as the lions got stuck into some serious fighting with their Christian victims.

This story is a neat analogy for the evolution of Latin – an ancient language that travelled across the world, had seemingly died and yet still blossoms today in the oddest of places. Never mind the fact that most of the people who now come across the flowers of Latin haven't the faintest idea that those flowers have their roots in that language.

Architecture, Roman numerals, satire, comedy, the right use of particular words… Once you can link up the modern incarnation with its Latin root, the rewards are thrilling.

In his Booker Prize-winning novel, *The Line of Beauty*, Alan

Hollinghurst described those people who know all the big turning points in history as being able to look back at the world as an enfilade of rooms: Greece gives way to Rome... Rome to the Byzantine Empire... the Renaissance... the British Empire... America... and so on.

Knowing a bit of Latin is an invitation to the biggest room in the building, with a view down the corridor to all the succeeding ages. And you can get your hands on that invitation at any age. Alfred the Great, who knew how crucial it was to learn Latin to become a civilised man, took it up in his 30s.

PROSECCO AND PISTACHIO – OR HOW TO READ THIS BOOK

My favourite guidebook is called *Venice for Pleasure* by J.G. Links. That is exactly what it does – shows you all the pleasure of Venice without any of the "Oh God, I ought to go to the Accademia at some stage and hoist in four million Tintorettos; but, Christ, I'd prefer a pistachio ice cream and a glass of prosecco."

J.G. Links's plan was not to show you the ice creams and proseccos (*siccus, -a, -um, adj.* – dry). He said you could find a café yourself; there are plenty of perfectly good ones all over Venice. The same went for the four million Tintorettos: you could get a high-brow *Blue Guide* yourself, full of dates and architectural glossaries. His plan instead was to take you for a lovely walk around the highlights and obscure golden corners of Venice, leaving you to do all the Tintorettos if and when you felt mentally strong enough.

Well, that's sort of the plan in this book. It would be vain to say that reading it will be as pleasant as walking round St Mark's Square after a pistachio ice cream and three glasses of prosecco. Lovely as Latin is, learning it is not all pleasure. As Molesworth, the heroically lazy schoolboy hero of Geoffrey Willans and Ronald Searle's 1950s book, says, "Actually, it is quite easy to be topp (sic) in lat. you just have to work."

Still, the point of this book is to make learning Latin as pleasurable as possible, allowing you to gently pick up (cf. split infinitives, p.125) the rudiments without feeling like an eleven-year-old faced with a long summer evening full of conjugations and declensions to memorise all over again.

All that daunting stuff is here: principal parts, locatives, ablative absolutes. And you *can* sit down and learn it all on long summer evenings if you want. But I've tried to make this a book you can read straight through, with the conjugations and declensions etc (*et cetera* – and the rest) sectioned off in boxes to be learned as you come across them, or later, or not at all.

Although I've used all those nightmareish expressions like conditional clauses and subjunctives, I've also called them things like "woulda/shoulda/coulda" words. Call it dumbing down if you like. If you think you're clever, just convert these patronising expressions back into conditional clauses and subjunctives or whatever. If you're happy being dumb, stick to the easy expressions.

I've also included some little chunks on Roman architecture and literature, but they really are little. There simply wasn't room here to do justice to Roman roads, underfloor heating and their million other contributions to modern civilisation.

Throughout the book, I have dropped in bits of vocabulary, marked **VOCAB.** In a slightly irritating way, to drum things in, I've also put in brackets the Latin derivation (*derivo, -are* – I derive) of certain words and explained Latin idioms that have crept into the language unexplained, i.e., when I write "i.e." I'll put (*id est* – that is) after it, when I use it for the first time.

But you don't have to work that hard. This book doesn't have all the declensions and conjugations that you'll ever need; for that you can go to the Latin equivalent of the Blue Guide, *Kennedy's Latin Primer*.

EATING SHORTBREAD ON THE BANKS OF LAKE GENEVA

My father likes to tell the story of the great fortunes made by the writers of Latin and Greek grammar books. There may never have been that many people doing Latin or Greek at any one particular time but every one of them needed a Lewis and Short dictionary and a Kennedy's *Shorter Latin Primer*. The

Primer was the *vademecum* (literally "go-with-me" – a crucial book you take everywhere with you) of the Latin-learning boy. And it was normally boys; it's still the case that more boys than girls tend to learn Latin and at an earlier age.

With its distinctive psychedelic, bleached-blue cover picture of the Colosseum and its ancient-looking font – as if a Roman sculptor had just finished carving it into a tablet – the *Primer* was a popular target for graffiti. With a few deft Tipp-Ex strokes, it was quickly transformed by a million schoolboys into Kennedy's *Shortbread Eating Primer*. Boys bought multiple copies because primers got so heavily mutilated and were often stolen because they were so vital.

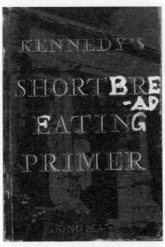

The book of books, written by the Shrewsbury headmaster, Benjamin Hall Kennedy, in 1875, revised by Sir James Mountford, Liverpool University's Professor of Latin, in 1930, and customised by me, aged ten

Anyway, so my father's story goes, the money made by the schoolmasters every year out of a fresh generation of eight-year-olds, and a staler generation of nine-year-old graffiti artists who had to replace their copies, was so vast that the masters decamped en masse to live in tax exile in vast, deep-eaved chalets by Lake Geneva. If you took a walk by a Swiss lake in the 1930s – the peak time for the writing of Latin grammar books – you could hardly fail to bump into knots of bespectacled millionaires swapping gags about ablative absolutes and rogue gerundives. Here, footling around in a rowing boat in the shallows of Lake Geneva, was Benjamin Hall Kennedy, the original writer of the *Primer*, in deep conversation over cognate accusatives with the man who revised it in 1930, Sir James Mountford. There was Liddell, deep in conversation over a gluhwein with Scott about the correct Greek word for the most terrible of Athenian punishments – "to stuff a radish up the fundament" (*raphanidosis*, by the way).

Even if my father's story exaggerates the takings for classics grammar books, it does uphold one basic truth: that those books have been in print for 70 years or more, a lot longer than plenty of books about living languages.

In 2004, Kennedy's *Primer* entered its 78th impression, and that was just of Sir James Mountford's 1962 edition. The original B.H. Kennedy edition went through dozens of further impressions. And the reason why they went through so many is that everything is there: every conjugation, declension, locative and correlative pronoun. There was no need for a new book.

So, as J.G. Links says in his guidebook, by all means keep a copy of the dry masterpieces to hand – in his case, the *Blue Guide*; in our case, the *Primer*.

The idea here is rather to give you a pleasurable breeze through the main principles of Latin without bringing on the blood, sweat and tears. Take in what follows and you should be able to negotiate all Latin sentences. This book has the crucial declensions and conjugations you need to know to build a skeleton of Latin knowledge on which Kennedy can fit the flesh.

The two books should complement each other and, if they do and popular success follows and little boys find it within their hearts to mutilate this book, I hope there's still space besides the shores of Lake Geneva to squeeze in another chalet.

In brief, if you already know the bare bones of Latin, by the time you've finished this book your dormant knowledge (*dormio, dormire* – I sleep) will have woken up.

And, if you have no knowledge, dormant or otherwise, you'll have the basics, which should mean you'll at least be able to translate this, the simple Latin – but all the more moving for that – of Leonardo Bruni's epitaph in the church of Santa Croce in Florence. (Bruni, by the way, was an eminent

Florentine humanist and classicist (1369-1444), best known for his Latin history of Florence, *Historiarum Florentinarum Libri XII*).

*The inscription on Bruni's tomb in
Santa Croce, Florence*

*Postquam Leonardus e vita migravit
Historia luget; eloquentia muta est
Ferturque musas tum Graecas tum
Latinas lacrimas tenere non potuisse.*

The translation is given on the last page of this book. Don't cheat by looking now.

Back to Basics – Sex, Cases and Word Order

How we laughed in 1981 when we were ten and learning Latin for the first time in 4 Pi, my class in my prep school, North Bridge House in Regent's Park. How silly it seemed that Romans actually talked the stuff we were learning. Lovely, patient and gentle as our Latin teacher, Mrs Pickersgill – Marilyn Monroe meets Miss Jean Brodie – was, Latin seemed by contrast, such a precise, concise, rigid language.

And it didn't help that all the Romans seemed to talk about, were *fossae* and *valla*, ditches and ramparts, and *sagittae* and *bella*, arrows and wars. We also had to learn so many declensions, conjugations and rules that it seemed extraordinary that you could ever master them well enough to have an easy-going chat about Ben Hur's chances in the 3.30, or whether Livia was really having an affair with Germanicus or not. And how on earth did they always remember what the verb in their sentences was and save it till the end?

On reflection, the reason Latin seemed such a strange language to chat in was not so much because of its strangeness as because it was dead. You can imagine people speaking much odder languages, like Finnish – which, like Estonian and Hungarian, is one of the few languages in Europe that doesn't share the Indo-European roots common to, among others, Latin, English, French, Frisian, Russian, Bengali, Hindi and Farsi. That's presumably because there are still lots of living Finns around, speaking Finnish. Latin, though, died before the age of recording – most surviving instances of it, apart from the cod Latin spoken in the Vatican and dialects surviving in the odd Swiss canton, are formal, preserved in deeply thought-out poetry, prose and documents. And yet of course it was a language that people once used to talk about the weather and their sex lives; people laughed and cried in Latin. The modern language which gives us the best example of what spoken Latin was like is Italian. Yes, that most hot blooded, passionate and angry of languages, is only a small jump from Latin.

English, on the other hand, is a bloody big jump from Latin. They are such different languages that a literal translation from one to the other sounds and looks very awkward, like putting a big foot in a small sock. English is not nearly as close a relative of Latin as French, and even French is a descendant through many generations. Kingsley Amis shows what a great chasm there is between Latin and French in an imaginary dialogue "between a scrounging legionary, perhaps a Vandal or a Parthian by origin, and a willing but benighted yokel [in ancient Gaul, which became France]":

LEGIONARY: (in vile Latin): I want water. Bring me water. Aquam.

YOKEL: Ugh?

LEGIONARY: Aquam! Say aquam, you bloody fool. Go on – aquam.

YOKEL: O? [To be spelt eau when they get to the writing stage centuries later.]

LEGIONARY: Bring it to the high cliff. The high cliff. Altum.

YOKEL: Ugh?

LEGIONARY: Altum! Say altum, you bumpkin. Go on – altum.

YOKEL: O? [To be spelt haut when etc.]

The English jump is a bigger stretch.

LEGIONARY: Our chaps are thinking of calling this place Eboracum. Go on, say it, you bog-trotter.

YOKEL: York?

Kingsley Amis on Latin

[*The King's English – A Guide to Modern Usage*, 1997]

It may be worth looking at how the English language developed, once the Romans left Britain to be conquered by the Angles and Saxons.

The language they brought with them, Anglo-Saxon, itself borrowed lots of words from Latin, either directly or via French. And then, when the Normans came, their brand of French imported even more Latinate words. Indeed over the centuries English was mutilated and diluted by all sorts of different languages that its incorporation of Latin was random and chaotic.

So, to say you need to understand Latin to understand English, as some people do say, is as crazy as suggesting that you need to understand Anglo-Saxon, German and Norman French to understand English. Knowing all those languages would certainly be helpful, but it's a bit much to ask.

The *really* useful thing about Latin is not so much that it will help you understand English as that it will help you understand Latin, in which some of the most stirring prose and poetry ever was written. Know Latin, and you will know world literature from the third century BC, when writers got going in Rome, through the so-called Golden Age of Latin – Lucretius, Catullus, Sallust, Cicero and Caesar – the Augustan Age – Ovid, Horace, Virgil and Livy – down to the end of the Silver Age in 120 AD – Martial, Juvenal, Lucan, Seneca, Pliny and Tacitus.

The only reason you will know English better as a result of reading Latin is because it is so different from Latin, not because of any similarities. It is in computing the changes from one language to another that you are forced to think about the structure of each of them.

It is also important to remember when writing Latin and translating it, that, though dead now and often preserved in stiff forms, it was once as malleable as English, and that it developed enormously in the 1500 years that it was in use. So do not treat it as a relic to be worshipped, as something to be translated word for word, or, if you're pompous, something to show off about; treat it rather as a way of reading, translating and writing beautiful and moving prose and poetry.

Before you start producing your free-flowing, honeyed words, though, you've got to know your way round some of the rigid-seeming oddities of Latin. And the first of these oddities is Latin word order.

I YOU LOVE – LATIN WORD ORDER

We put our verbs in the middle of our sentences – "I send batches of flowers hourly to Cameron Diaz". The Romans like to put the verb at the end, as in: "I batches of flowers hourly to Cameron Diaz send." So the traditional Latin word order is

Subject Object Verb, or SOV if you want a not particularly inspirational mnemonic.

Latin small talk – Asterix the Gaul (1969)

SOV is a pretty good rule of thumb, but you can play around with it, as lots of Romans, and especially poets, did. Virgil wrote his own epitaph for his tomb in Naples and went wild with his word order:

Mantua me genuit; Calabri rapuere; tenet nunc
Parthenope; cecini pascua, rura, duces.

Mantua gave birth to me; The Calabrians took me away; now Naples [or Parthenope, its anthropomorphic name, from the Greek for "maiden-face"] holds me; I sang of fields, farms and leaders.

Even though you won't necessarily be able to translate this, you can see that the subject jumps around in each clause. *Mantua* and *Calabri* are in the traditional position, at the beginning of the clause. *Parthenope* is at the end while *cecini*, the verb – "I sang"– is at the beginning of its clause, English-style. I'd say stick to the SOV rules but just be aware that they can be played around with.

SEX IN ANCIENT ROME

The three Latin sexes or, better, genders are masculine, feminine and neuter. We have the same ones – he, she and it. The difference is that practically all our nouns are neuter. We call a cucumber "it" and you call a soul "it", where the Romans considered cucumbers (*cucumis,-eris*) masculine and souls (*anima, -ae*) feminine.

The Latin approach to these things is not as annoying as it might at first seem. It soon becomes second nature that words which end in *-us* (like *dominus* and *Augustus*) are masculine; *-a* words (like *mensa, Diana* and *Camilla*) are feminine; and *-um* words (like *bellum, pilum, castrum*) are neuter, with a minority that don't have this nice and easy pattern to them. The other thing that becomes second nature is that adjectives should agree with nouns, i.e. masculine nouns take masculine adjectives, feminine nouns, feminine adjectives, etc. Plural nouns also take plural adjectives. This can provide comfortable room for showing off in English; e.g. the plural of *persona non grata* – an unwelcome person – is *personae non gratae.*

The neuter adjective is a wonderfully pliable thing. On its own, it can be used to mean an object with the qualities of that adjective. So *nigrum* means "black", but it also means "a black thing". That "thing" is itself fairly pliable and can be twisted to mean "circumstance". As a result, *in extremis* literally means "in extreme things", but it also means "in extreme circumstances" and ended up being popularly used to mean "on the verge of death".

THE CASES – OR CHURCHILL'S PROBLEMS WITH A TABLE

Now that you've worked out Latin word order, it's time to deal with the cases that each of those words – subject, object and the rest of them – go into. There are six cases in Latin. Here they are with their role attached:

Nominative – The case that the subject in a sentence takes.

Vocative – The case of the person or thing that is addressed.

Accusative – The case that the object of the verb takes.

Genitive – The case that signifies possession. When something belongs to someone, that someone is in the genitive, their position usually signified by the word "of". So in "the Bride of Frankenstein", "Frankenstein" goes in the genitive; in "the girl of my best friend", "my best friend" goes in the genitive; in "the *plume de ma tante*", "*ma tante*" goes in the genitive.

Dative – When something is done "to" or "for" someone or something, that person or thing goes in the dative: "Everything I do, I do it *for* you." (Bryan Adams, 1991)

Ablative – When something is done "by", "with" or "from" someone or something, the person or thing is in the ablative: "By God's grace ["grace" in the ablative], with the right rubbing alcohol ["rubbing alcohol" in the ablative], from any decent ironmonger's ["decent ironmonger" in the ablative], I shall be drunk by dusk."

Here are all the cases, embedded in Hamlet's speech to Rosencrantz about how miserable he is:

"I [the subject, in the nominative] have of late – but

wherefore I know not, Rosencrantz [person you're talking to, in the vocative] – lost all my mirth [the object of
the verb, in the accusative], forgone all custom of exer-
cises; and indeed it goes so heavily with my disposition
that this goodly frame, the earth, seems to me [anything
"to" or "for", in the dative] a sterile promontory, this
most excellent canopy, the air, look you, this brave o'er-
hanging firmament, this majestical roof fretted with
golden fire [anything "by", "with" or "from" – in the
ablative], why, it appears no other thing to me than a
foul and pestilent congregation of vapours [anything
"of", in the genitive]."

(By the way, I added in the "Rosencrantz" to get a vocative).
Now that you have got the meaning behind the six cases,
you need to know how to form them, hence the First
Declension, using the noun *mensa, mensae, f.* – table.

	Singular	Plural
NOM.	*mensa*	*mensae*
VOC.	*mensa*	*mensae*
ACC.	*mensam*	*mensas*
GEN.	*mensae*	*mensarum*
DAT.	*mensae*	*mensis*
ABL.	*mensa*	*mensis*

The First Declension: always ends in -a, mostly feminine

33

The mere mention of the words *mensa, mensa, mensam...* will bring on the sweats in some people. God, the hours spent learning all those lists. And, Christ, the pointlessness!

That's certainly what Winston Churchill thought when he was learning Latin at Harrow in the late 1880s.

Stupid boy – Churchill at Harrow

The method of teaching Latin at Harrow was the same then, as now: rote learning of tables; in this case, literally. Churchill was asked by his Latin master to decline *mensa*, meaning "table". Churchill was confused as to how it was possible that the same form, *mensa* could be used in three different ways: why it was the same in the nominative, vocative and ablative.

Here he describes the incident in his autobiography:

"Then why does mensa [in the vocative] also mean 'O

table'?" I inquired, "and what does 'O table' mean?"

"Mensa, 'O table', is the vocative case," the master replied.

"But why 'O table'?" I persisted in genuine curiosity.

"'O table' – you would use that in addressing a table, in invoking a table."

And then seeing that he was not carrying me with him: "You would use it in speaking to a table. If you are impertinent, you will be punished and punished, let me tell you, very severely," was his conclusive rejoinder.

Winston Spencer Churchill,
My early life (1930)

Churchill had a point. You'd never address a table, except perhaps to swear at it, when you stub your toe. And, even then, you'd use it in conjunction with a swearword (*Sanguinea mensa* – "Bloody table"). Nevertheless, all nouns have a vocative, inanimate or not.

The consoling thing is that, except for when you're addressing people, you'll hardly ever come across the vocative. The other consoling thing is that the vocative is practically always exactly the same as the nominative, so it's hardly worth learning it.

Annoyingly, we're now going to come across one of the few

exceptions to this rule – Second Declension nouns – where the vocative, ending in *-e*, is different to the nominative. There are two types of Second Declension masculine nouns – those ending in *-us* and those ending in *-er*. The *-us* nouns go like *dominus*. The *-er* nouns go like *magister*.

	Singular	Plural
NOM.	*dominus*	*domini*
VOC.	*domine*	*domini*
ACC.	*dominum*	*dominos*
GEN.	*domini*	*dominorum*
DAT.	*domino*	*dominis*
ABL.	*domino*	*dominis*

The Second Declension: ending in -us

	Singular	Plural
NOM.	*magister*	*magistri*
VOC.	*magister*	*magistri*
ACC.	*magistrum*	*magistros*
GEN.	*magistri*	*magistrorum*
DAT.	*magistro*	*magistris*
ABL.	*magistro*	*magistris*

The Second Declension: ending in -er

The name of the game, dominoes, is obscurely derived from *dominus*, meaning master. The hoods worn in 1710 by Italian priests – grand figures, considered a type of master – were called dominoes. Black with holes cut into them for the eyes, their name got passed on to the black rectangular playing blocks with their white dots.

This connection between dominus and dominoes wouldn't immediately spring to the mind of even the greatest Latinist; I've just had to look it up.

The distance between the two words is enough to show that a knowledge of Latin doesn't necessarily unlock the secret of lots of obscure Latinate words.

In fact, it's a good idea to try to avoid Latinate words when translating Latin. This isn't just because Latin words don't always translate into similar-sounding Latinate English words. It's also that, for all the beauty of Latin, Latinate words in English are often clumsy and pompous as you should find out in the next chapter.

George Orwell, Berks and Wankers –
or How to Translate Latin into Lovely
English

When it comes to translating Latin into English, the real joy comes in doing what Latin teacher after Latin teacher begged you to do – "Be more imaginative, Mount. Who's ever said, 'Sejanus, needing to be promoted, enjoined the centurions to go by, with or from home? Much better to say, 'Sejanus was so desperate to curry favour with the emperor that he ordered all the centurions to quit the city by nightfall or he'd have their balls skewered on the Traitors' Gate of Tiberius's Palace by sunrise.'"

Here is Orwell, on the potential pitfalls of translation:

Bad writers, and especially scientific, political, and sociological writers, are nearly always haunted by the notion that Latin or Greek words are grander than

Saxon ones, and unnecessary words like expedite, ameliorate, predict, extraneous, deracinated, clandestine, subaqueous, and hundreds of others constantly gain ground from their Anglo-Saxon numbers.

"The jargon peculiar to Marxist writing (hyena, hangman, cannibal, petty bourgeois, gentry, lackey, flunkey, mad dog, White Guard, etc.) consists largely of words translated from Russian, German, or French; but the normal way of coining a new word is to use a Latin or Greek root with the appropriate affix and, where necessary, the size formation. It is often easier to make up words of this kind (deregionalise, impermissible, extramarital, non-fragmentary and so forth) than to think up the English words that will cover one's meaning. The result, in general, is an increase in slovenliness and vagueness... The inflated style itself is a kind of euphemism. A mass of Latin words falls upon the facts like soft snow, blurring the outline and covering up all the details.

George Orwell,
Politics and the English Language (1946)

This doesn't mean that, as Orwell acknowledges, good writing is simply a matter of having as few Latinate words as possible, and exchanging them for Anglo-Saxon ones.

Sometimes, particularly with new and scientific words, the

Latinate word is the only choice. You might even *want* that extra touch of pomposity and archness that the Latinate words brings.

But on the whole Orwell was right. A too-literal use of Latin leads to a constipated use of English.

Kingsley Amis debates the danger of this constipated English in his last, posthumously published, book, *The King's English – A Guide to Modern Usage* (1997), where he divides English language pedants into Berks and Wankers:

BERKS are careless, coarse, crass, gross and of what anybody would agree is a lower social class than one's own. They speak in a slipshod way with dropped Hs, intruded glottal stops and many mistakes in grammar. Left to them the English language would die of impurity, like late Latin.

WANKERS are prissy, fussy, priggish, prim and of what they would probably misrepresent as a higher social class than one's own. They speak in an over-precise way with much pedantic insistence on letters not generally sounded, especially Hs. Left to them the language would die of purity, like medieval Latin.

You come across very few Berks in the modern Latin-reading world, and a lot of Wankers.

Wankers have a proprietorial attachment to archaisms, mostly used by those who want to send out the strong signal – "I-know-this-clever-thing-and-you-don't." Wankers will insist on a correct use of Latin in English when it actually ends up sounding ridiculous. For e.g.,

> "Do you think that people like me who know Latin tend to be *genii* who should be heard more often in *auditoria?*"
>
> "No, I think most geniuses would think you were a bit of a Wanker and would not want to bloody go near any auditoriums where there was any danger of you turning up."
>
> "Not 'to bloody go'. You've split an infinitive there. 'To go near any bloody auditoria' is better."

I rest my case.

Chris Patten, the former MP and Governor of Hong Kong, now the Chancellor of Oxford University, was guilty of classic Wanker's Latin in a review of a history of Balliol College by John Jones in *The Spectator* (January 14, 2006): "The foreword to this edition by the university's recent Vice-Chancellor and Balliol's quondam Master, Colin Lucas," wrote Lord Patten, "draws attention to Balliol's recurrent capacity for being out of tune with the prevailing orthodoxy of the times."

Quondam? *Quondam?*

As a basic rule of thumb you immediately qualify for Wanker's status if you use a Latin word when an English one would do fine. *Quondam* means "former" and there would have been absolutely zero effect lost if Lord Patten had written "Balliol's *former* Master, Colin Lucas", but then he wouldn't have got that all-important patina (no pun intended in this word, itself a bit of Wanker's Latin, *patina, -ae f.* – a dish or plate, and thus synonymous with the thick green film of oxidation that develops on bronze surfaces) of supposed intelligence and sophistication that comes with using Latin where plain English will do.

Funnily enough, Sir Kingsley's own son, Martin, comes across as a bit of a Wanker in a row the two men once had about the correct use of the word "dilapidated".

The surprisingly literal-minded Martin insisted that dilapidated should only be used in its exact sense: cf. *lapis, lapidis m.* – stone, and the verb *dilapido, -are* – to remove stones, from which the past participle *dilapidatus* – having had stones removed. So Martin was saying that you should really only use the word in the sense of, "I wish that articulated lorry hadn't careered into that dry-stone wall; it now looks very dilapidated." You could, Martin conceded, use it metaphorically, but only if you had the proper sense in mind.

So – "The Colosseum is looking a bit dilapidated these days," but not, "Kirk Douglas is looking a bit dilapidated these days," because he isn't actually missing any physical part of him, however ropey he might appear.

THE WANKER'S PITFALL

Interestingly, if you use the exact translation of the bit of Latin that an English word is derived from, you are often both a Wanker and *wrong*.

It would be fairly silly, for instance, to insist on using "nebulous" to mean "misty" or "foggy" purely in the meteorological sense of the original Latin adjective (*nebulosus, -a, -um*). And no one could possibly understand you if you used "strata" to mean "blankets", "saddle-cloths" or "pavements", as the Romans did (*stratum, -i, n.*).

That doesn't mean that it isn't intriguing to know the Latin origin of English words, or that it isn't useful show-off material. In fact, the greater the jump in meaning, the more esoteric you'll seem if you can explain the jump without, like a Wanker, becoming attached to the original meaning.

So, while it isn't surprising that *candidus, -a, -um adj.* means "white" and that candid, i.e. "pure, unvarnished", is derived from it, the jump to "candidate" is less obvious. The word "candidate" evolved from the fact that Roman candidates for election wore togas covered in white chalk dust to make them stand out in a crowd.

Just as odd is the derivation of *atrium* meaning, as it did in Latin, "a hall". Atrium is derived from *ater, atra, atrum adj.* – black, since the atrium was where the main, wall-blackening fire in a house was.

The Atrium, Greenwich Village, New York – not black

Yes, indeed: being too literal in your English can lead to all sorts of nastiness – not just lots of complicated Latinate words, but also clunky, leaden sentences: "The pirates, bearing malice, will have borne weapons against the soothsayers."

The genius at capturing this stilted idiocy is Molesworth, hero of the Geoffrey Willans and Ronald Searle books. Molesworth gets the constipated feel of badly translated Latin spot on:

The Gauls have attacked the camp with shouts they hav frightened the citizens they hav killed the enemy with darts and arows and blamed the belgians. They have also continued to march into Italy. Would it not be more interesting if they did something new?

In her bestselling novel, *The Secret History*, Donna Tartt captures that same awful, literal clumsiness when the narrator, Richard Papen, exhausted by the strain of murdering his classmate, copies a friend's second-rate translation: "Being weary from the march, the soldiers stopped to offer sacrifices at the temple. I came back from that country and said that I had seen the Gorgon, but it did not make me a stone."

That said, for all Tartt's and Molesworth's brilliance in hammering the stunted English that comes from literal translation, there is often beauty in the brevity of the original Latin.

On a sundial in a monastery cloisters on the edge of Venice, an old monk once inscribed: *Horas non numero nisi serenas.* It means literally, "I don't count the hours unless they are serene ones." But it really means, "When I come to die, the only moments that matter will have been the moments when I was at ease." And the joy of the original is increased when you say it out loud. For all its brevity, when you say, "*Horas non numero nisi serenas,*" it sounds like what it is – a rich, distilled, romantic language – the purest, headiest Italian.

There are times when Latin use in English is not Wankerish, but right. On two occasions, on one day – January 20th, 2006 – the *Daily Telegraph* comment page used Latin in a precise, illuminating way that worked better than the equivalent English would have.

First, Tom Utley used his Latin in writing about the story in the *Sun* that Fathers 4 Justice, the group that lobbies for greater access to children for divorced fathers, were planning to kidnap the Prime Minister's son:

> So the fascinating question arises of who, exactly, wanted that story to appear on the front page of the *Sun*? *Cui bono*? – as detectives and lawyers used to ask, in the days when Latin was taught more widely than cake decoration in our schools. Who benefits? The first answer, obviously, is the *Sun*. Sensational stories sell newspapers – and, sure enough, the *Sun*'s front page was the only one that BBC2 thought worthy of attention on Wednesday's *Newsnight*.

Then, on the same day, in the *Telegraph*'s first leader, discussing the Prime Minister's plans for greater selection in schools, the leader-writer wrote:

Other countries have shown how publicly funded but privately-run schools can raise standards for the worst off. One effect, *pari passu*, is that schools become responsible for checking the backgrounds of their own staff.

Tom Utley, formerly/quondam of the Telegraph, now of the Daily Mail, fine classicist

In the first extract, *cui bono* is nicer-sounding and more powerful than the English equivalent – "Who benefits?"

Cui bono also has an added nuance, for those who are familiar with the phrase: it encapsulates the idea of some hidden, often underhand, benefit that you have to do a bit of detective work to discover. N.B. (*nota bene*, note well) in what a masterly way Mr Utley here avoids the charge of being called a Wanker, by explaining the use of the expression, i.e. he doesn't do the real Wanker's thing of leaving something in Latin that a lot of readers won't get, in order to show off and say, "I know what this means and you don't, naa-naa-ner-naa-naa."

In the second extract, the leader-writer again uses a Latin expression, *pari passu*, that sounds much more stylish and less clumsy than its English equivalent – "at the same pace", "being treated in the same way". So, here, the leader-writer is saying with these two Latin words, that, "Schools – *pari passu/ being publicly funded and privately run* – become responsible for checking the backgrounds of their own staff."

You at the Back, Pay Attention

Anyway, it's time for some more grammar, in particular Second Declension neuter nouns, ending in *-um*, as in *bellum, -i, n.* – war (as in bellicose). Pronounce "*bellum*" as "blum", and you get the nice little rhythm, "Blum, blum, blum, bli, blo, blo; bla, bla, bla, bllorum, blis, blis." Just in case this doesn't make any sense, take a look at the full table below.

	Singular	Plural
NOM.	*bellum*	*bella*
VOC.	*bellum*	*bella*
ACC.	*bellum*	*bella*
GEN.	*belli*	*bellorum*
DAT.	*bello*	*bellis*
ABL.	*bello*	*bellis*

Second Declension nouns: ending in -um

48

The nice thing about all neuter nouns and adjectives is that they are the same in the nominative, vocative and accusative, and the same goes for neuter plurals.

THE GREAT MOUNTS – OR THIRD DECLENSION NOUNS

On the dedication page of this book, I've actually got it wrong in calling my brother and sister, Mons Maximus and Mons Maxima. Let me explain how these nicknames came about.

For a long time, between 1976 and 1982, my elder brother, William, my younger sister, Mary, and I were all at the same schools, North Bridge House Junior and Senior School, in Hampstead and Regent's Park respectively. And there we started learning Latin.

Mons Maximus, Mons, Mons Maxima

For a while, in the early days, we enjoyed rude Latin with phrases like *ubi sub ubi* ("where", "under", "wear" – say it quickly); and our favourite made-up verb – po, pis, pist, pimus, pistis, pants (say it quickly).

We then graduated to giving each other Latin names. I got called Mons (as in *mons, montis, m.* – a mountain). In a couple of pages you'll see how to decline *mons*.

For a few years at prep school, I was just straightforwardly "Mons". But, if my brother, my sister and I had been at an old-fashioned prep school, we would have been Mons maior, Mons minor and Mons minima. My dedication rather ignores the correct hierarchy of age and salutes instead my siblings' shared brilliance of character – *Mons Maximus*, the Greatest Mount (masculine), and *Mons Maxima*, the Greatest Mount (feminine).

You might call this terrible Latin because *mons* is masculine and should never really take a feminine adjective. In any case, my brother and sister should really be in the dative because the book is dedicated *to* them as in "To [or for] William and Mary". So the dedication should read *Monti Maiori et Monti Minimae*, or even, with the Mounts in the plural, *Montibus Maiori et Minimae* but that doesn't sound as fittingly grand as *Mons Maximus et Mons Maxima*.

I got the gender of *mons* wrong again and also got the wrong tense – and was also a bit of a Wanker – when I wrote an inscription on a bit of Welsh slate to hang over the Flemish fireplace in the ruined, overgrown cottages cleared out by my parents next to their unruined cottage in St Twynnells, Pembrokeshire.

"The Great Mounts tamed these Sylvan Ruins, April 1993"

But back to the Third Declension, which in the case of *mons* goes like this:

	Singular	Plural
NOM.	*mons*	*montes*
VOC.	*mons*	*montes*
ACC.	*montem*	*montes*
GEN.	*montis*	*montium*
DAT.	*monti*	*montibus*
ABL.	*monte*	*montibus*

A Third Declension noun

There are lots of irregular Third Declension nouns so it's

not really worth spending too much time going into.

A good rule of thumb is to count on the nominative being pretty different from the accusative – that's when it jumps into its longer form if it's going to, and then after that it pretty much settles into the familiar rhythm.

By the way, if you want to start forming English words out of these expanding Third Declension nouns – like *rex, regis,* and *mons, montis* – that get bigger in the genitive, then you take the root from the longer accusative form: mountain, not mounsain; regicide, not rexicide.

The suffix, '-icide', is a useful one, to be added on to anything that's in danger of being murdered. Aborticide is a new word much in vogue among the American religious right. It is derived from *caedo, -ere, cecidi, caesum* – I kill.

As ever there are exceptions to the expanding-noun rule. Sometimes a noun gets smaller in the accusative. *Iuppiter* – Jupiter – goes: *Juppiter, Jovem, Jovis, Jovi, Jove.* From which you will see that when Bertie Wooster was heard to swear, "By Jove", he was really uttering a bit of a tautology, since Jove (the ablative form of the noun) means "By Jupiter" in the first place.

Actually, it's worth having a look at Roman gods...

DIANA THE HUNTRESS AND CAMILLA THE VIRGIN: ROMAN GODS AND GODDESSES

Swearing oaths: Asterix the Gaul

René Goscinny and Albert Uderzo, the author and artist respectively of the Asterix books, are here, as so often in their books, spot-on about the little details of the Roman Empire – in this case religion. One of the priorities of Roman colonisation was the appropriation of the local gods that were worshipped by the tribes they conquered.

In the little unconquered Brittany village where Asterix and Obelix lived in 50 BC, the Gauls would certainly have worshipped Toutatis, the ancient god of war, fertility and wealth, before they were conquered. The conquering Romans then gradually introduced some of their own customs – gods, baths, togas, as they did in Roman Britain (*infra*, below).

And little by little, as this top-down influence seeped through the colonies, the lower orders began to imitate their chiefs. There was therefore no need for the Romans to inflict any nasty compulsive conversion: the native gods and habits of the conquered were painlessly absorbed into the new Roman tradition. And the Romans themselves borrowed from previous empires and from the places they colonised. The stories of Hercules were culled from the Greek tales of Heracles and they, in turn, had been borrowed from the stories that pre-Greek tribes had concocted about their own local strong man.

Christianity ended up doing the same with many of its rituals. Christmas is a joint appropriation of the Roman winter festival, Saturnalia, celebrating Saturn, the god of agriculture, and the northern pagan ritual, known as Yule. Yule was a celebration of the birth of the pagan Sun God, Mithras (much appropriated by Roman Britons), and was observed on 21 December, the shortest day of the year, when Yule logs were burnt, and kisses exchanged as a fertility ritual under the mistletoe, the crucial ingredient in Getafix's magic potion in the Asterix books.

Getafix and the Magic Potion

It wasn't until 350 AD that Pope Julius I declared that Christ's birth would be celebrated on December 25, making it as easy as possible for pagan Romans, the vast majority of Romans, to switch to the new rituals.

With this cross-fertilisation between empires and religions, it is no coincidence that the Greek and Roman gods and their powers and stories are so interchangeable.

Here's a list of the main Greek gods and goddesses and their Roman equivalents:

Zeus/Jupiter – King of the Gods, free with his lightning bolts.

Poseidon/Neptune – God of the sea.

Hades/Pluto – God of the underworld.

Hestia/Vesta – Goddess of the Hearth, symbol of the home, worshipped by the Vestal Virgins.

Hera/Juno – Jupiter's wife and, confusingly, sister.

Ares/Mars – God of war.

Athena/Minerva – The motherless daughter of Zeus who sprang fully-formed from his head. The goddess of wisdom; thus London's club for dons and vicars, the Athenaeum.

Apollo/also Apollo – God of the sun. Often depicted with his chariot galloping along, bringing the dawn with him.

Aphrodite/Venus – The goddess of love.

Hermes/Mercury – The fleet-footed messenger god, associated with newspapers.

Artemis/Diana – Goddess of the moon and hunting. Thus the conclusion to Earl Spencer's funeral tribute to his sister (who, unlike Camilla Parker Bowles, didn't like hunting much) in Westminster Abbey on September 6th, 1997:

> It is a point to remember that of all the ironies about Diana, perhaps the greatest was this – a girl given the name of the ancient goddess of hunting was, in the end, the most hunted person of the modern age.

Camilla in Roman legend was, by the way, a virgin queen

of the Volscians, the daughter of King Metabus. She helped Turnus in his conflict with Aeneas, and was killed in the process.

In the following passage in Book XI (11, cf., Roman numerals, *infra*) of Virgil's *Aeneid*, the goddess Diana describes the death of Camilla, the little royal Amazon with a love of virginity, and explains how she has always loved her:

> *"Graditur bellum ad crudele Camilla,*
> *O virgo, et nostris nequiquam cingitur armis,*
> *Cara mihi ante alias." Neque enim novus iste Dianae*
> *Venit amor subitaque animum dulcedine movit.*

> "And so Camilla went off to that cruel war;
> She was kitted out with all my weapons but in vain.
> She was dearer to me than anyone else."
> Diana's love for Camilla wasn't anything new –
> It wasn't as if this was the first time that this love had
> stirred Diana's soul with sweetness.

Aeneid, Book XI

VOCAB.
gradior, gradi, gressus sum – I walk
nequiquam – in vain
cingo, cingere, cinxi, cinctum – I surround, encircle

subitus, -a, -um – sudden

dulcedo, inis f – sweetness

More gods:

Hephaestus/Vulcan – Son of Hera, God of Fire. The only ugly and deformed god. Makes armour and weapons forged in volcanoes.

Gaea/Terra – Mother Earth.

Asclepius/Aesculapius – God of medicine.

Cronos/Saturn – God of agriculture.

Demeter/Ceres – Goddess of grain.

Dionysus/Bacchus – God of wine and vegetation.

Eros/Cupid – God of love.

Hypnos/Somnus – God of sleep.

Rhea/Ops – Wife of Cronus/Saturn. The mother goddess.

Uranus/also Uranus – God of the sky and father of the Titans.

Nike/Victoria – Goddess of Victory. Incidentally, if you want to be a real Wanker, pronounce the popular sports shoe brand as the ancient Greeks did – *Kneekay*.

Anyway, it's time to get back to the nitty-gritty:

FOURTH DECLENSION NOUNS

These are only a little more tricky than the Third Declension, the principal pitfall being the fact that they end in *-us*, like Second Declension nouns, i.e. *dominus,* but are declined in an entirely different way.

	Singular	Plural
NOM.	*vultus*	*vultus*
VOC.	*vultus*	*vultus*
ACC.	*vultum*	*vultus*
GEN.	*vultus*	*vultuum*
DAT.	*vultui*	*vultibus*
ABL.	*vultu*	*vultibus*

Fourth Declension nouns

Corinthian Columns and the Historical Importance of Carry on Cleo – a quick cultural tour of Rome

To get a rapid hold of Roman architecture, you must learn a rude mnemonic – DICC.

DICC may be the sort of thing taught to you by the annoying teacher who wants you to like him by taking advantage of the adolescent's obsession with sex and his amusement at rude words.

Still, remember DICC, and you have the boilerplate for all classical architecture from 600 to the present day.

Doric, Ionic, Corinthian and Composite columns – that is, DICC – are the four literal pillars of Roman buildings, although it must be acknowledged that the principles are almost entirely borrowed from the Greeks. DICC gives you the chronology of the orders of architecture – Doric came first, then Ionic, then Corinthian, then Composite. They also grow taller and their capitals (their crests) get more ornate, the later they get. And, whenever you get a classical building of more than one floor, the types of column run through the DICC order, the higher you go, i.e. Doric on the ground floor, Ionic on the first etc.

DORIC COLUMNS – SEVENTH CENTURY BC

A Doric column

The Doric column was thought to be perfected under Dorus, the ruler of the Peloponnese, who built a temple in the style in Argos, dedicated to Juno.

It is the simplest, chunkiest and thought to be the most male order, and was said by Vitruvius, the first architectural historian, to be derived from the ratio of the length of a man's foot to his height.

A Doric column gradually tapers to the top, bulging outwards as it does so, in an architectural trick called entasis. If the line were straight, the eye would tend to think the column was collapsing inwardly; thus the need to compensate in the other direction.

Doric columns are topped with a simple, unadorned round capital. The columns tend to be fluted – that is, they have vertical grooves running up and down them. The best-known examples are the best-known columns in the world, the socking great ones on the Parthenon in Athens.

Male columns: the Doric Parthenon, Athens

IONIC COLUMNS – SIXTH CENTURY BC

An Ionic column

Thought to be the most feminine of orders, the Ionic order is best spotted through its spreading capital with two scrolls, or volutes, unfurling on either side of it; or, if you prefer, like a girl's curls tucked up on either side of her head.

Ionic columns, like girls, are thin; thinner than the bulky Doric columns. They are about nine times taller than they are wide.

The Ionic order came from the Ionian colonies of Greece on the south-western shores of Asia Minor (modern Turkey). Its finest example is again on the Parthenon, in its side temple – the Erechtheum.

Like pretty young girls: Ionic columns at the Erechtheum, Athens

A Corinthian column

The Corinthian column was first used by the Greeks in 400 BC but was much popularised by the Romans.

The Corinthian capital, heavier and more ornate than its predecessors, was the first to use acanthus leaves sprouting out of the side, with small volutes folding out at the top.

From Roman temple to Christian church: the Corinthian portico of the Pantheon, Rome

The best-known Corinthian temples are the Pantheon (built 120 AD) and the Temple of Castor and Pollux in the Forum, both in Rome.

*Rome's favourite twins: the Corinthian temple of
Castor and Pollux in the Forum*

Incidentally, the shallow curve of the roof of the Pantheon is so sophisticated that modern architectural historians still don't know how it was built.

Incidentally, again, Castor and Pollux were the twin gods who Romans thought they saw at their victory over the Etruscans in 496 BC. As a result, the Romans built an early version of this temple in the Forum; it was later rebuilt by the Emperor Tiberius in 6 AD.

A Composite column

The Composite column, the showiest of them all, was the only one actually invented by the Romans, with the upper part of the capital based on the Ionic capital, and the lower part on the Corinthian; thus the word Composite.

The first example of the Composite order is on the Arch of Titus, in the Roman Forum, built in 82 AD.

A purely Roman building: Composite columns
at the Arch of Titus, Rome

Real swots might also want to take in the Tuscan order, which wasn't invented until the sixteenth century by Italian architectural theorists. This is the simplest order of all, basically a Doric column with a base and no fluting. Because it was so simple to build, the Tuscan column was called gardener's Doric, easily knocked up to make gateposts and fences.

Architects looking for a simple, consciously ancient effect, often plump for the Tuscan order. This was the look Inigo Jones went for in St Paul, Covent Garden, with its Tuscan pillars and heavy overhanging eaves. The church appears in the opening scenes of the film *My Fair Lady*. Indeed it is under the Tuscan eaves of St Paul that Professor Higgins meets Eliza Doolittle.

St Paul, Covent Garden

Roman architecture was so advanced that it wasn't bettered for a thousand years, until the twelfth century when the French came up with the pointed Gothic arch, which could bear more weight and therefore support taller buildings than previously possible.

It's no coincidence, then, that an alternative word for Norman architecture in Britain is Romanesque – the fact is that William the Conqueror's builders hadn't advanced on the principles of Roman architecture by the time they invaded Britain. And the earliest Norman buildings in Britain – the chapel in the Tower of London, St Bartholomew's in the City of London, Durham Cathedral – with their round arches and barrel vaulting could all have been built a thousand years earlier in Rome.

In fact, the very shape of our churches is dictated by Roman architecture and, more precisely, by Roman temples. The idea of a cross-shape was of course a debt to Jesus and the cross. But the concept of a long rectangular nave flanked by aisles, with a semi-circular chancel at the end where the altar is, comes from pre-Christian Roman temples.

If you take a walk down Queen Victoria Street in the City of London, you'll find the second century AD Temple of Mithras, originally built underground and now raised on a platform, so commuters flooding in from Cannon Street can get a good look at it.

Temple of Mithras, London

Mithras was the god of light and sun, worshipped for slaying a primordial bull in a dark cave – thus the tendency to build Mithraea, as a group of temples to Mithras are called, underground – and unleashing the powers of creativity and life in the world.

The nave bit was where Romans, like us, gathered for services, although they tended to sit in the aisles on benches that ran alongside the walls. And the chancel area (from *cancellus, - i, m.* – the railing or screen before the altar) was where sacrifices were burnt in Roman pagan rituals.

The Norman chancel in St Bartholomew's, Smithfield

The influences of Roman architecture on British and western architecture are too deep and numerous to mention beyond the obvious examples: the triumphal arch (as in Marble Arch) derived from the Arch of Titus in the Roman Forum; the triumphal column (as in Nelson's Column) from Trajan's Column in Rome; modern running tracks from the stadium at Rome; theatres from Marcellus's theatre in Rome…

There is one particular Roman building, though, which is worthy of a special mention – the second century BC Temple of Vesta in Rome which inspired not only St Paul's Cathedral in London, St Peter's in Rome and the Radcliffe Camera in Oxford but every dome on a colonnaded drum in the world.

The Temple of Hercules, Rome,
the inspiration for St Paul's Cathedral

This temple was once thought to be the Temple of Vesta,

originally inhabited by the famous Vestal Virgins – the only female priests in Rome. Their main job was to maintain the sacred fire of Vesta, goddess of the hearth; thus the name Swan Vestas, matches that wouldn't go out easily.

And incidentally, the Vestal Virgins were not that different from the version portrayed in *Carry on Cleo*. Just as in the film, Vestal Virgins tended to be young – they started in the temple at any age from three to ten – and were in good physical condition, chosen as they were from grand families, though they presumably got a bit ropey after their 30 years of service, with the first ten spent as novices, the second ten as Vestal Virgins proper, and the last ten as supervisors.

At this point, they were permitted to leave the temple and marry. And Bridget Joneses everywhere will be consoled by their story: even though they were at least 33 when they left the temple, they were considered an excellent catch.

Useful secondary source

The virgins had special privileges: they could look after their own property; they had special seats at the games, while other women had to sit in the back row; and they were generally considered sacred. If a condemned man met a Vestal Virgin on his way to the scaffold, he was pardoned automatically. All this was dependent on them remaining virgins, as *Carry on Cleo* rightly stresses. If they broke their vow of chastity, they were buried alive – to spill a Vestal Virgin's blood was forbidden, even after she'd lost her virginity – in the Campus Sceleratus, the "Wicked Fields", while their lovers were flogged to death. The Vestal Virgins survived until 394 AD, when all non-Christian cults were outlawed.

By the way, the Temple of Vesta and the other buildings I have been talking about in Rome are all on or around the Seven Hills of Rome. If you are not familiar with this area, you ought to know that only one of these ancient seven hills of Rome, the Capitoline Hill, properly strikes you as a hill when you go round the city. They were much more obvious as hills before the marshy ravines between them were drained and filled in with buildings.

THE SEVEN HILLS OF ROME

Aventine Hill – The hill where Remus chose to live.

Caelian Hill – The Belgravia of Rome during the Roman Republic, 510-31 BC.

Capitoline Hill – The hill of government, as in Capitol Hill in Washington. The temples of Jupiter Optimus Maximus, Juno Moneta, and Concord were all on the Capitoline.

Esquiline Hill – a quiet hill.

Palatine Hill – Romulus's Hill, where he founded the city after killing his twin brother, Remus. Rome may not have been built in a day, but it was certainly founded by Romulus on a specific one, April 21st, 753 BC.

Quirinal Hill – Now home to the Quirinal Palace, a sixteenth-century papal palace, the residence of the kings of Italy from 1870-1946 and since then home to the Italian president.

Viminal Hill – another quiet hill.

Fifth Declension Nouns

These are thin on the ground, but those that do crop up tend to crop up a lot. The most familiar are *dies, diei f.*– day and *res, rei f.* – thing. *Res* is a tricky word. The classic translation is "thing" but actually that's usually the last thing it means.

It can mean "matter", particularly when used in the ablative, as in "*re*", meaning "in the matter of". This is a use seemingly now confined to office memos: "Re paperclips on the eleventh floor conference room: HR are using too many of them."

Perhaps a better all-purpose word for *res* is "affair", as in *respublica*, meaning public affairs, coming to mean the state. The proper name for the Roman state was *Senatus Populusque Romanus* – "the Senate and the Roman People" (*que*, when tagged onto the end of a noun, means "and", whereas *et*, the more general word for "and", is used to connect clauses and phrases – confusingly).

Senatus Populusque Romanus is neatly shortened to *SPQR*, the words stitched into every legionnaire's tassel-edged flag, when he sailed across the Channel to Pevensey in Sussex to invade England. The letters are still all over Rome, on monuments, cab doors and drain covers.

Drain pride – Via Luigi Santini, Trastevere, Rome

A rebus, by the way, is a representation of a word or a phrase by symbols: i.e. two gates and a head are the municipal shorthand rebus for Gateshead on town hall buildings in the north-east. It is derived from the expression, *Non verbis sed rebus* – "Not by words, but by things".

And here is how to decline *res*:

	Singular	Plural
NOM.	*res*	*res*
VOC.	*res*	*res*
ACC.	*rem*	*res*
GEN.	*rei*	*rerum*
DAT.	*rei*	*rebus*
ABL.	*re*	*rebus*

A Fifth Declension noun

THE GERUND

Gerunds and gerundives are held up as the oddest thing about Latin because, some claim, there is no English equivalent.

Kingsley Amis says of the gerundive, "Fowler says there is no gerundive in English, only a participle. He writes 2000 words on the gerund alone. In my experience you will not get very far with the gerund or the gerundive unless you know Latin, nor a great deal further if you do."

I'm not sure if either Fowler or Sir Kingsley are right.

The gerund is a verbal noun, i.e a way of turning a verb into a noun: so the gerund of "I love" is "loving" and the gerund of "I do" is "doing". In "Making love is quite an art", "making love" is a gerund.

Making gerunds (another gerund, incidentally) is perfectly easy. You simply add *-ndum* to the end of a verb, to get:

> *amandum – loving*
> *monendum – showing*
> *regendum – ruling*
> *audiendum – hearing*

The gerund

All of these gerunds decline like the noun *bellum, -i, n.* – war. For e.g.:

Quid mihi tam multas laudando, Basse,
puellas mutatum domina cogis abire mea?

Why are you forcing me to chuck my mistress and change her, Bassus, by praising [*laudando* – gerund] so many other girls?

Propertius, *Elegies IV*

VOCAB.

laudo, -are – I praise
puella, -ae f. – girl
muto, -are – I change
domina, -ae f. – mistress
cogo, -ere, coegi, coactum – I force
abeo, -ire, -ii, -itum – I go away

The gerundive is a little more confusing but all the more wonderful when you know it.

It's a verbal adjective, meaning, "*needing* to be kissed/ electrocuted/glued", and, as a verbal adjective, declines like a normal adjective, i.e. *magnus, -a, -um adj.* – great.

---

amandus, -a, -um – needing to be loved
monendus, -a, -um – needing to be warned
regendus, -a, -um – needing to be ruled
audiendus, -a, -um – needing to be heard

The gerundive

A gerundive is used in a precisely Latin way in English by John Mortimer's Rumpole of the Bailey, who knows some classics, and calls his wife, "She who must be obeyed."

The name Amanda is also a gerundive, meaning "A girl that must be loved."

"Agenda" is strictly a gerundive, from *ago, agere, egi, actum* – "I do, carry out". So "agenda" literally means "things that need to be done". If you wanted to be a Wanker, and there was only one item to be dealt with at your next annual general meeting, you could quite correctly say, "What an interesting agendum we have before us today."

The gerundive can also be used to mean "I must... massage/giggle/whatever" when you add it to the verb "to be":

Nunc est bibendum
"Now, we must drink" (literally, "it is to be drunk")
Horace, Odes 18,
The Blessings and Dangers of Wine

Nunc est bibendum indeed...
and maybe a little Latin learning, too

BERTIE WOOSTER'S CLASSICAL EDUCATION – LATIN IN ENGLISH LITERATURE

To trace the influence of Latin on English literature would take a longer and more serious book than this.

Enough, then, to point to the three great Latin influences on English literature: first, the great number of storylines taken from Roman myth and Roman history (which had an equally vast effect on Renaissance painters and sculptors); secondly, the classical education that most educated men had in Europe from 1100 AD to 1900; and finally, Christianity.

Take Shakespeare. Ben Jonson said he had "small Latin and less Greek", but even Shakespeare, a man of relatively humble origins who didn't go to university, did know a little of both.

Shakespeare's education at the King's New School in Stratford-upon-Avon would have consisted almost entirely of translating Latin into English and vice versa. His principal text book would have been William Lily's *Short Introduction of Grammar*, authorised by Henry VIII as the only grammar book to be used in schools.

It's no surprise, then, that Shakespeare's plays are full of classical stories, history and references. *Julius Caesar, Coriolanus, Antony and Cleopatra* and *Titus Andronicus* are the most obvious examples. *The Comedy of Errors* was even based on a Roman comedy, Plautus's *The Twin Brothers*.

I could go on. Dante, Milton, Dryden, Pope, Samuel Johnson – Latin translations and Roman myths and histories were the wellspring of much of their work. Renaissance and Reformation comedy got so tangled up with its Latin roots that writers started recasting – and Christianising – classical texts to suit the moral and religious outlook of the day.

Schonaeus's *Terentius Christianus* took the place of the original Terence in classrooms. Alexander Nowell drafted new prologues for Terence's *Eunuchus* for performance at Westminster School in 1545, turning bawdy scenes of prostitution into moral examples of how not to behave. As he wrote,

Hinc meretricum sordes, ingluviem rapacitatem nullo periculo, multa cum utilitate tamenque voluptae minori cognoscas, et ubi noris perpetuo oderis.

You'll learn about filthy tarts from this play, their gluttony and greed, but with no danger; instead it'll be incredibly useful and enjoyable because once you've heard all about it, you'll hate it for ever.

For half a millennium up until the nineteenth century, Latin was the mark of the educated man, and an Oxford education meant a classical education.

In Oxford in the seventeenth century, a lazy undergraduate

called Tom Brown (1663-1704) was on the verge of being sent down, when John Fell (1625-1686, Dean of Christ Church and Bishop of Oxford) offered to spare him if he could translate a Martial epigram on the spot.

Here is Martial's couplet, followed by Brown's ex tempore ("from the time", off the cuff) translation:

Non amo te, Sabidi, nec possum dicere quare;
Hoc tantum possum dicere, non amo te.

I do not love thee, Doctor Fell,
The reason why I cannot tell;
But this alone I know full well,
I do not love thee, Doctor Fell.

Good old Dr Fell let Tom stay on, only for him to drop out later and fail to take his degree.

ECCE, JEEVES

This mingling of Latin into the education of English writers and their works went on at full tilt until a century ago.

In his recent biography, *Wodehouse – A Life* (2004), Robert McCrum wrote about the extreme influence of classics on the writer, who won a senior classical scholarship at Dulwich School in 1897.

In 1969, McCrum reports, an Oxford classicist wrote to Wodehouse after he'd noticed a similarity between Terence's *The Self-Tormentor* and Wodehouse's *The Luck of the Bodkins*. The undergraduate asked him if Plautus or Terence had been an influence.

Wodehouse wrote back, "There certainly is a great resemblance between the two passages, and it can only be explained by a similarity of thought between us, for though in my time at Dulwich we read a great many authors, for some reason neither Plautus nor Terence came my way. Why would this be? Because P and T were supposed to be rather low stuff?... But we read Aristophanes who was just as slangy as either of them."

Certainly Bertie Wooster is forever drawing from the classical education he had at Harrow and Eton at the turn of the nineteenth century. As Bertie says in *Right Ho, Jeeves* (1934), "This done, I retired to an armchair and put my feet up, sipping the mixture with carefree enjoyment, rather like Caesar having one in his tent the day he overcame the Nervii."

And, in *The Girl on the Boat* (1922), Wodehouse gives a Latin lesson that wouldn't disgrace the most fastidious of classics masters:

Nothing is more curious than the myriad ways in which the reaction from an unfortunate love affair manifests itself in various men.

No two males behave in the same way under the spur of the female fickleness. Archilochum, for instance, according to the Roman writer, *proprio rabies armavit iambo*. It is no good pretending out of politeness that you know what that means, so I will translate. "*Rabies* – his grouch – *armavit* – armed – *Archilochum* – Armilochus – *iambo* – with the iambic – *proprio* – his own invention."

In other words, when the poet Archilochus was handed his hat by the lady of his affections, he consoled himself by going off and writing satirical verse about her in a new metre which he had thought up immediately after leaving the house. That was the way the thing affected him.

THE LATIN-RITE CHURCH

The Old Testament may have been written in Hebrew, the New in Greek, but it was in Latin that the medieval priest principally read and in Latin that he spoke in church.

It is in the translation from the Latin, too, that worshippers were used to hearing the liturgy. That was before the *Book of Common Prayer* was edged out by the 1980 *Alternative Service Book* and the 2000 *Common Worship* series.

Confusingly, the Latin Church used a Greek liturgy for several hundred years before adopting Latin, but it was the Latin version that stuck until Vatican II in 1962-5.

Vatican II pushed the Catholic liturgy away from direct use of Latin and from translations that remained faithful to the original Latin. How gratifying then that John Paul II reversed the trend when he signed off the 2001 directive, known as *Liturgiam Authenticam,* demanding translations that were closer to Latin.

In America, Australia, Scotland, England and Wales, bishops have now voted to accept the Vatican-backed translations.

So, in America for example, the prayer before communion, which had gone "Lord, I am not worthy to receive you," now goes "Lord, I am not worthy that you should enter under my roof." That's much closer to the original Latin – "*Domine, non sum dignus, ut intres sub tectum meum.*"

Likewise, in the Nicene Creed, "born of the Virgin Mary" will revert to "incarnate of the Virgin Mary" ("*incarnatus…ex Maria Virgine*").

And, in the exchange between priest and congregation:

Priest: "The Lord be with you."
Congregation: "And also with you."

will become:

Priest: "The Lord be with you."
Congregation: "And with your spirit.."

Priest: "*Dominus Vobiscum.*"
Congregation: "*Et cum spiritu tuo.*"

To all the Sirs I've loved Before –
Latin teachers I have known

Almost twenty years after I left the classroom, I realise that Latin teachers are not the dry, old sticks I thought they were when I was filled with the cynical idiocy of youth. Latin teachers may grow old and dusty, and they may take to tank tops and brown flared suits by the time they have taught classics for twenty years in a minor public school on the fringes of Tring.

But they remain romantics.

I never saw my last prep school Latin teacher, Dr Rutherford, so transported to a different era, and to a deeper chamber of his soul, than when he read out the Catullus poem that he must have recited to the upper sixth for 25 autumns in a row, after games, just before dusk on a Thursday afternoon.

We had been playing football on the frozen mud pitches in the shadow of the mosque where Baker Street meets Regent's

Park. Back at the school – a white stucco Nash terraced house by the park – my little twelve-year-old fingers were so cold that it was hard to do up the buttons on my white shirt and knot my turquoise tie in the few minutes we had before Dr Rutherford came through the door.

A bachelor in his mid-30s who had never got the don's job at Cambridge he had coveted as an undergraduate, he was a volatile man whose moods shifted from anger at having to teach half-dressed twelve-year-olds (although I don't think he minded the half-dressed bit) to joy at being able to link his job to his love of Latin.

"Christ, why aren't you ready yet, Upper 6 EJ?" Dr Rutherford shouted as he came through the door.

"Sorry, sir," said Aron Lowder, the class hard man who combined a shrewd understanding of man's behaviour with a lack of interest in his intellectual achievements, "Any chance of some Catullus while we finish dressing?"

"Don't be insolent, Lowder," said Dr Rutherford, his face softening, "We're due to do Cincinnatus and his plough today, and that's what we'll do, but, since Mount is still bare-chested, I suppose there's time…"

"Oh wicked, sir!" said Aron, leaning back in his chair, and flicking off the switch of his mind for the next five minutes.

"*Vivamus, mea Lesbia, atque amemus,*" began Dr Rutherford, his hands tucked behind his back, his eyes staring out of the Regency window, fixed on the Nash villas of Park Village East, where Sven-Goran Erikkson and Nancy dell'Olio now live,

"Rumores-que senum severiorum
omnes unius aestimemus assis.
soles occidere et redire possunt:
nobis cum semel occidit brevis lux,
nox est perpetua una dormienda.
da mi basia mille, deinde centum,
dein mille altera, dein secunda centum,
deinde usque altera mille, deinde centum.
dein, cum milia multa fecerimus,
conturbabimus illa, ne sciamus,
aut ne quis malus invidere possit,
cum tantum sciat esse basiorum."

Here is Ben Jonson's translation:

Let's live and love: To Lesbia

Let us live, my Lesbia
and let us judge all the rumours of the old men
to be worth just one penny!
The suns are able to fall and rise:

When that brief light has fallen for us
we must sleep a never-ending night.
Give me a thousand kisses, then another hundred,
then another thousand, then a second hundred,
then yet another thousand more, then another hundred.
Then, when we have made many thousands,
we will mix them all up so that we don't know
and so that no one can be jealous of us when he finds
out how many kisses we have shared.

When Dr Rutherford got to the crux of the poem – "Give me a thousand kisses, then another hundred…" "*Da mi basia mille, deinde centum, dein mille altera,*" (Say it out loud, and you'll see what I mean) – he might have been a whip-thin Italian ragamuffin on the backstreets of Naples serenading a Norwegian Valkyrie in a bikini on her year-off; not a 35-year-old bachelor in a Viyella shirt and Harris tweed jacket.

Even more extraordinary, *mirabile dictu* ("wonderful to say", but say it out loud, and hear how much lovelier it is in Latin), he could do all this while his angry gaze was transferred to Cotgrove minor at the back of the class, engrossed in applying sideburns, mullet and baseball cap to the profile of Virgil on the front of his *Aeneid I* textbook.

I'm sure that Rutherford had once dreamt of saying the same lines, when he was not much older than Cotgrove minor, to the unattainably lovely peach in the sixth form, or perhaps even to a girl at the girls' school down the road.

I have had several types of classics teacher. However broken down they've been, however thick the layers of dandruff flakes on their shoulders, however deeply buried in them the lissome eighteen-year-old who once lisped Catullus snippets to a lover, horizontal in the back of a punt on the Cam, they all held on to a passion for Latin...

***

Richard Conner – a brilliant Cambridge scholar in his late 40s, who'd had a car crash shortly before coming to teach at my prep school and still had a forehead pockmarked with cuts. Mr Conner had a Darwinian view of individual capabilities.

"Lowder," he barked one morning, "You'll never get the hang of Horace. Much better use of your time to come up here and pick the scabs off my forehead."

"Everyone else, '*Dulce et decorum est.*' What does it mean, Fussell?"

"Erm, not entirely sure, sir."

This brilliant man then turned his bloody forehead away from Lowder and in the direction of London Zoo.

Eyes glazed and focused on the middle distance, he recited Horace softly, translating as he went, line by line, to twelve, transfixed, thirteen-year-old boys.

Lowder crept back to his chair. Even Cotgrove minor, who had by now spent a year turning the cover of his *Aeneid* into a Woodstock scene – with Virgil on stage accompanied by Janis Joplin – stopped colouring in Virgil's dangly pearl earring.

"*Dulce et decorum est pro patria mori:*
mors et fugacem persequitur virum
nec parcit inbellis iuventae
poplitibus timidove tergo."

"How sweet and lovely it is to die for your country,
And death pursues even the man who flees
Nor spares the hamstrings or cowardly backs
Of battle-shy youths."

"Of course, bloody Wilfred Owen ripped the line off for his poem, *Dulce et Decorum Est*, in 1917. Got shot a fortnight before the Armistice. Serves him bloody right. That's what happens to boys who plagiarise. COTGROVE! That means you. And Virgil would never have worn a batik scarf."

Still you sensed that Mr Conner did care at least a little for Owen, as he continued:

"Bent double, like old beggars under sacks,
Knock-kneed, coughing like hags, we cursed through
                                        sludge,
Till on the haunting flares we turned our backs
And towards our distant rest began to trudge.
Men marched asleep. Many had lost their boots
But limped on, blood-shod. All went lame; all blind;
Drunk with fatigue; deaf even to the hoots
Of tired, outstripped Five-Nines that dropped behind."

Mr Conner was now shouting at us,

"Gas! Gas! Quick, boys! – An ecstasy of fumbling,
Fitting the clumsy helmets just in time;
But someone still was yelling out and stumbling,
And flound'ring like a man in fire or lime...
Dim, through the misty panes and thick green light,
As under a green sea, I saw him drowning.
In all my dreams, before my helpless sight,
He plunges at me, guttering, choking, drowning.
If in some smothering dreams you too could pace
Behind the wagon that we flung him in,
And watch the white eyes writhing in his face,
His hanging face, like a devil's sick of sin;
If you could hear, at every jolt, the blood

Come gargling from the froth-corrupted lungs,
Obscene as cancer, bitter as the cud
Of vile, incurable sores on innocent tongues,
My friend, you would not tell with such high zest
To children ardent for some desperate glory,
The old Lie; Dulce et decorum est
Pro patria mori."

"Owen didn't think much of Horace, did he? But what do you think, boys? Is it a lie? Is it a lie of Mrs Thatcher to send the Task Force to the Falklands? Well is it, Cotgrove? I'll give you a clue. NO, IT BLOODY WELL ISN'T!"

***

Dr Cedric Meadows – an Old Etonian scholar, the spitting image of John Le Mesurier, with all the distractedness, style and slight despair of Captain Wilson in *Dad's Army*, plus a dose of anger thrown in at the shortcomings of thirteen-year-olds.

"Oh Lowder, you're incorrigible. What's that from, boys? Keiko?"

"Erm, *corrigo* – I correct, sir," said Hiroshi Keiko, a silent Japanese boy who only opened his mouth to give perfect answers to teachers, in Maths, Latin, Physics, Chemistry,

French and English comprehension, but not, thank God, in English composition, since Keiko lacked any capacity for individual thought.

"Therefore incorrigible means?" asked Dr Meadows.

"Incorrectible, sir?"

"Good. But more colloquial, please... Mount?"

"Unchangeable?"

"Not quite right..."

"Intolerable?"

"Better..."

"Unbearable."

"Spot on, Keiko. Gold star for being so clever."

Under his breath, Lowder whispered to Keiko, across the classroom, "Wanker, wankeris. Third Declension, masculine. Meaning? *You.*"

***

Roger Harvey – an avuncular teacher, who taught so many subjects – Latin, Greek, Russian, General Studies – that it was unlikely that he was ever going to be an expert in any of them.

"Sir, sir. When do you use the infinitive to mean 'to do' something and when do you use the subjunctive?"

"Ah, excellent question, Warshaw. Very, very easy to slip up on this one. Sometimes you need to use the infinitive to mean 'to do' something; sometimes you use the subjunctive."

"Yes, sir, but I still don't quite get it."

It is the Mr Harveys of this world, who love teaching but haven't actually got much to teach, who are the easiest to lure away from work. Molesworth is the master of the type:

"What is the use of latin sir?"

    "er well er quite simple molesworth. latin is er classics you kno and classics are – well they are er – they are the studies of the ancient peoples. er latin gives you not only the history of Rome but er (happy inspiration) its culture, it er tells you about interesting men like J.Caesar, hannibal, livy, Romulus remus and er lars porsena of clusium."

Of all these school masters, Rutherford was perhaps the closest we got to that model classics teacher – the one who never married, because he is married to his subject; the one who, if he did marry, might take advantage of the new civil partnership dispensation adopted by Sir Elton John and David Furnish in December – although we neither knew nor cared about his sexual inclinations then.

Our parents might have made a quick mental calculation, balancing Dr Rutherford's brilliance as a teacher against his penchant for playing duets with boys on the grand piano squeezed into his bachelor flat, before deciding, "Well, if Harry gets into Winchester, he'll come across plenty more people like that, any way."

My parents certainly couldn't have cared less when I told them one evening what Dr Rutherford had told me that afternoon after our Latin prose class.

"Do you know, Mount, how I judge whether I like people?"

"No, sir."

"Well, I think about playing a duet with them and, do you know, sometimes, when you're playing a duet with somebody, you have to reach round their back to hit the high notes?"

"No, sir."

"Well, I'd feel very uncomfortable reaching round the back of, say, Mr Harvey."

"Yes, sir."

"But I'd feel perfectly at ease playing a duet with you, Mount."

"'Fraid I don't play the piano, sir."

"That's not really the point…"

Dr Rutherford's desires – for Latin, and for the boys who studied it – may have been strong but he generally did his best to conceal them behind a cold, hard exterior. Occasionally, he would adopt a consciously laddish pose – "Phwoarrh, I saw *The Dukes of Hazzard* over the weekend, boys. That Daisy Duke…"

It was Dr Rutherford who gave me my first glass of sherry – some warm fino, after Greek poetry – at the age of twelve. It was Dr Rutherford who first took me, and a group of thirteen-year-olds, to Athens – "Inhale the taste of ancient Greece," he boomed above the traffic choking the Plaka at the foot of the Acropolis.

The Rutherford type – warm, soft heart behind stiff, unforgiving tweed – has a long ancestry, beloved of journalists, novelists and playwrights.

As William Rees-Mogg said in the *Mail on Sunday* in May, 2005, talking about his daughter's bid to become Tory MP for Aberavon, "Country people are not modern, classical schoolmasters are not modern, manufacturers are not modern, particularly if they are involved in heavy industry, the Welsh are not modern. Certainly Aberavon is not modern, and the people suffer because of it."

The classics master is a quick literary shortcut to encapsulating a lonely, highly intelligent man dedicated to his subject, and often to his pupils. They are never in fiction – and rarely in real life – female. They are often dons manqués – men who, due to a personality fault, or an unfortunate incident with a boy, never made it as academics. And so they become, like Dr Rutherford, substitute dons at school, keen on building up one-to-one relationships with the pupils and dismissive of their contemporaries in the school common-room.

There was a lot of Rutherford in Andrew Crocker-Harris, "The Crock", in Terence Rattigan's *The Browning Version*, a crusty, short-tempered classics master in a serge suit and a stiff collar, cuckolded by his younger, pretty wife. The crust is broken when a boy gives him Browning's translation of Aeschylus as a present and he bursts into tears:

ANDREW, *left alone, continues for a time staring at the text he has been pretending to read. Then he puts one hand over his eyes. There is a knock on the door.*

ANDREW: Come in.

TAPLOW *appears timidly from behind the screen.*

[Sharply] Yes, Taplow? What is it?

TAPLOW: Nothing, sir.

ANDREW: What do you mean, nothing?

TAPLOW: I just came back to say goodbye, sir.

ANDREW: Oh. [*He gets up*]

TAPLOW: I didn't have a chance with the head here. I rather dashed out, I'm afraid. I thought I'd just come back and – and wish you luck, sir.

ANDREW: Thank you, Taplow. That's good of you.

TAPLOW: I – er – thought this might interest you, sir. [*He quickly thrusts a small book into Andrew's hand*]

ANDREW: What is it?

TAPLOW: Verse tranlsation of the *Agamemnon*, sir. The

Browning Version. It's not much good, I've been reading it in the Chapel gardens.

ANDREW *very deliberately turns over the pages of the book.*

ANDREW: Very interesting, Taplow. [*He seeems to have a little difficulty in speaking. He clears his throat and then goes on in his level, gentle voice.*] I know the translation, of course. It has its faults, I agree, but I think you will enjoy it more when you get used to the metre he employs.

He hands it to TAPLOW *who brusquely thrusts it back to him.*

TAPLOW: It's for you, sir.

ANDREW: For me?

TAPLOW: Yes, sir. I've written in it.

ANDREW *opens the flyleaf and reads whatever is written there.*

ANDREW: Did you buy this?

TAPLOW: Yes, sir. It was only second-hand.

ANDREW: You shouldn't have spent your pocket-money this way.

TAPLOW: That's all right, sir. It wasn't very much. The price isn't still inside, is it?

ANDREW *carefully wipes his glasses and puts them on again.*

ANDREW: [*at length*] No. Just what you've written.

Nothing else.

TAPLOW: Good. I'm sorry you've got it already. I thought you probably would have –

ANDREW: I haven't got it already. I may have had it once. I can't remember. But I haven't got it now.

TAPLOW: That's all right, then.

ANDREW *continues to stare at* TAPLOW's *inscription on the flyleaf.*

[*Suspiciously*] What's the matter, sir? Have I got the accent wrong on eimenos?

ANDREW: No. The perispomenon is perfectly correct.

He lowers the book and we notice his hands are shaking from some intense inner effort as he takes off his spectacles.

In Evelyn Waugh's short story, *Scott-King's Modern Europe* [1947], Mr Scott-King, a lonely classics master, makes for the perfect victim of the cruelties of the modern world – "Growing slightly bald and slightly corpulent, known to generations of boys first as 'Scottie', then of late years, while barely middle-aged, as 'old Scottie'; a school 'institution', whose precise and slightly nasal lamentations of modern decadence were widely parodied."

After a lifetime of teaching dreary boys way below his intellectual level, he is delighted by what looks like the highlight of his career: an invitation to an obscure Eastern

European country, Neutralia, to give a lecture on the obscure poet that he knows more than anyone else in the world about, the seventh-century Latin poet, Bellorius.

Scott-King's ultimate disappointment, as he is humiliated and destroyed by the petty, evil ways of his totalitarian hosts, is of a piece with his life, and of a piece with the fictional expectation of all classics masters.

The American classics experience is not so intense but, even there, the caricature exists. In Donna Tartt's *The Secret History* (1992) , the classics master is single, obsessive, intellectual, overly-devoted to his pupils, fogeyish. His pupils in turn become so devoted to classics that they end up reenacting Bacchic rituals and murdering the class dork in the process.

The teacher in the book, Julian Morrow, was in fact based on a real-life teacher of Tartt's, Claude Fredericks, a well-connected bachelor of independent means with his own private printing firm, the Banyan Press. Born in 1923 and still alive at the time of writing, Fredericks only taught the pupils he wanted to teach – among them Bret Easton Ellis – at Bennington in Vermont, America's most expensive university, forming very close friendships for life, particularly with his male students.

The Svengali-like teacher encouraged an other-worldly life devoted to the mind, fine dressing and fine food. Easton Ellis referred to the coterie, and echoed the plot of *The Secret*

History, in *The Rules of Attraction* – "That weird group of Classics majors stand by, looking like undertakers… probably roaming the countryside sacrificing farmers and performing pagan rituals."

For all their devotion to ancient ritual, though, the classics students in *The Secret History* aren't much good at Greek. At one stage, an eighteen-year-old pupil – admittedly the dim murder victim, Bunny Corcoran, says,

"Ablative's the ticket. The hard ones are always ablative."

A slight pause.

"Bunny," said Charles, "You're mixed up. The ablative is in Latin."

"Well, of course, I know that," said Bunny irritably, after a confused pause which seemed to indicate the contrary, "but you know what I mean. Aorist, ablative, all the same thing, really…"

Looking back, I now feel the romance that pulses through the thin, dry veins of these devoted classics masters. It is a romance forged from this strange combination – of rigid rules of language coming up against the passionate, orgiastic, murderous history and literature of Italy when Italy was as romantic as it is now, but also happened to rule the world.

A decade of one's youth in dusty classrooms spent rote-learning those clinical rules while, as Dr Rutherford might have put it, inhaling the bloody, erotic, tragic, funny, distinctly unclinical taste of the ancient world, does not go away.

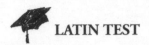 **LATIN TEST**

Every now and then, as I said, I am going to throw in a small test of your Latin skills so far, and here I think it would be good to see if you can decline *respublica*.

Respublica is declined as two words separated and then joined together, i.e. *res* is declined like *res*, and *publica* like *mensa*. Below is the correct declension. See if you can do it yourself, before turning it upside down to have a peek.

	Singular	Plural
NOM.	respublica	respublicae
VOC.	respublica	respublicae
ACC.	rempublicam	respublicas
GEN.	reipublicae	rerumpublicarum
DAT.	reipublicae	rebuspublicis
ABL.	republica	rebuspublicis

Little and Large – and Other Adjectives

Now, it's time for some pretty relentless tables of adjectives. The annoying thing is that there's no real way round needing to know adjectives. The good thing is, they're pretty easy to learn.

Helpfully, most adjectives go like *dominus* in the masculine, *mensa* in the feminine and *bellum* in the neuter. Let's start with *bonus, -a, -um* meaning "good".

	Masculine	**Feminine**	**Neuter**
NOM	*bonus*	*bona*	*bonum*
VOC	*bone*	*bona*	*bonum*
ACC	*bonum*	*bonam*	*bonum*
GEN	*boni*	*bonae*	*boni*
DAT	*boni*	*bonae*	*bono*
ABL	*bono*	*bona*	*bono*

First and Second Declension-type adjective: singular

	Masculine	**Feminine**	**Neuter**
NOM	*boni*	*bonae*	*bona*
VOC	*boni*	*bonae*	*bona*
ACC	*bonos*	*bonas*	*bona*
GEN	*bonorum*	*bonarum*	*bonorum*
DAT	*bonis*	*bonis*	*bonis*
ABL	*bonis*	*bonis*	*bonis*

First and Second Declension-type adjective: plural

Because of this similarity between adjectives and nouns, Pope Gregory was able to make the world's first bad pun, when he spotted some gorgeous blond English slaves in the Roman forum:

"Get those boys over there! Who the bloody hell are they?" asked Pope Gregory.

"Oh those," said a stall-holder, "They're Angles [that is, Englishmen, from *Anglus, -i*]."

"Non Angli [not Englishmen]," said Pope Gregory, barely able to control himself, "Sed angeli [but angels]."

By the way, adjectives usually go after the noun they're describing, as in:

Paulus Gasconius ebrius – A drunk Paul Gascoigne (*ebrius,-a, -um adj.* – inebriated).

Or:

Sheryla Gasconia bella – A beautiful Sheryl Gascoigne.

The next lot of adjectives end in *-is* for both masculine and feminine, and *-e* for neuter. An example of an adjective that goes like this is *mirabilis, -is, -e* (as in *annus mirabilis* – a wonderful year – an expression used for any year in which a lot of extraordinary things happen). The year of 1809 is the archetypal *annus mirabilis* – the birth year of Tennyson, Gogol, Charles Darwin, Abraham Lincoln and William Gladstone.

	Masculine/Feminine	**Neuter**
NOM	*mirabilis*	*mirabile*
VOC	*mirabilis*	*mirabile*
ACC	*mirabilem*	*mirabile*
GEN	*mirabilis*	*mirabilis*
DAT	*mirabili*	*mirabili*
ABL	*mirabili*	*mirabili*

Third Declension-type adjective: singular

	Masculine/Feminine	**Neuter**
NOM	*mirabiles*	*mirabilia*
VOC	*mirabiles*	*mirabilia*
ACC	*mirabiles*	*mirabilia*
GEN	*mirabilium*	*mirabilium*
DAT	*mirabilibus*	*mirabilibus*
ABL	*mirabilibus*	*mirabilibus*

Third Declension-type adjective: plural

In one of the Queen's wittier moments, she adapted the idiom in 1992 to *annus horribilis* – a bloody terrible year, when Windsor Castle burnt down, and the marriages of Prince Charles, Prince Andrew and Princess Anne fell apart.

The sub-editors at the *Sun* also showed all the benefits of a classical education during the Christmas of 2005, or MMV, as they'd know to call it.

The Queen had plumped for a serious Christmas broadcast, concentrating on the tsunami of the Christmas before and the Pakistan earthquake that year, and avoiding sugary reminders of Zara Phillips flashing her tongue-stud outside Sandringham Church or any mention of Camilla Parker Bowles. The *Sun* interpreted this as a slight to the new Duchess of Cornwall and so came up with the dream headline: Snubbus Horribilis. Quite grammatically correct, of course.

Tabloid Latin

It's from the neuter singular nominative of *mirabilis* that we get the saying, *mirabile dictu,* i.e wonderful to say – a phrase TO BE DROPPED INTO CONVERSATION LIBERALLY, often with heavy-handed irony: "Prince Charles has finally said, *mirabile dictu*, that, after all, it's not too bad living in a London palace and a Gloucestershire country house with half of Cornwall, mortgage-free, to fall back on."

From the same formation, you get *mirabile visu* – wonderful to see, and *horribile dictu* – horrible to say. Also to be used with irony – "*Horribile dictu*, the Carshalton guys have seen fit to give me a 70 grand bonus and a company MX5."

There are all sorts of variants on the *mirabilis, -is, -e* form, but they are minor ones. All that really differs is the nominative form and how it changes in the accusative. Once you've got to the genitive, they all pretty much follow mirabilis.

So, *celeber* – famous (thus celeb, a rare example of a Latin word shrinking in English, rather than being expanded) goes to *celebrem* in the accusative and, after that, it's *mirabilis* all over again: *celebris, celebri, celebri* etc.

That doesn't mean that all adjectives ending in *-er* go like *celeber*. Some, annoyingly, go like dominus, e.g. *miser* – miserable, which goes *miser, misera, miserum*.

There's no way of saying which way these adjectives will jump – whether they'll follow *miser* or *celeber*. Your best bet, apart from learning how they all go, is to take a gamble on them going like *miser*, until you gradually become more familiar with the ways of individual words.

Any adjective with an odd-sounding ending, like *felix* or *ingens,* will end up going like *mirabilis*, once it's made the jump to becoming a "fat accusative". So *felix* jumps to *felicem, felicis* etc, and *ingens* to *ingentem, ingentis* etc.

COMPARATIVES AND SUPERLATIVES

Now is as good a time as any to deal with these customers, which are nice and easy.

The simple rule of thumb is that, if you want to make something "more" whatever, add on *-ior*; and if you want to make it the "mostest" something, add on *-issimus*. So *stultus* – stupid, becomes *stultior* (more stupid), and then becomes *stultissimus* (stupidest)

The same goes for those odder adjectives which sound like Third Declension nouns, i.e *tristis, -is -e adj.* – sad, which goes *tristior, tristissimus.* As far as declining goes, comparatives go like Third Declension nouns and the superlatives go like *bonus, -a, -um.*

	Masc/Fem		Neuter
NOM	*stultior*		*stultius*
VOC	*stultior*		*stultius*
ACC	*stultiorem*		*stultius*
GEN		*stultioris*	
DAT		*stultiori*	
ABL		*stultiore*	
NOM	*stultiores*		*stultiora*
VOC	*stultiores*		*stultiora*
ACC	*stultiores*		*stultiora*
GEN		*stultiorum*	
DAT		*stultioribus*	
ABL		*stultioribus*	

Comparative Adjectives – stultior – more stupid

	Masculine	**Feminine**	**Neuter**
NOM	*tristissimus*	*tristissima*	*tristissimum*
VOC	*tristissime*	*tristissima*	*tristissimum*
ACC	*tristissimum*	*tristissimam*	*tristissimum*
GEN	*tristissimi*	*tristissimae*	*tristissimi*
DAT	*tristissimi*	*tristissimae*	*tristissimo*
ABL	*tristissimo*	*tristissima*	*tristissimo*
NOM	*tristissimi*	*tristissimae*	*tristissima*
VOC	*tristissimi*	*tristissimae*	*tristissima*
ACC	*tristissimos*	*tristissimas*	*tristissima*
GEN	*tristissimorum*	*tristissimarum*	*tristissimorum*
DAT	*tristissimis*	*tristissimis*	*tristissimis*
ABL	*tristissimis*	*tristissimis*	*tristissimis*

Superlative adjectives: tristissimus – saddest

An annoying little irregularity creeps in for *mirabilis*-type words, however. If the Queen were to have an even worse year than 1992, it would be an *annus horribilior*, as you'd imagine. But, if she were to have the worst year of all time, she'd double her l's, as it were, and have an *annus horribillimus*.

On the horrid old principle of 'the more regularly used, the more irregularly spelt', the adjectives you'll use most take the oddest comparatives and superlatives:

Bonus – good	*melior* – better	*optimus* – best
		(thus "optimist")
Malus – bad	*peior* – worse	*pessimus* — worst
		(thus "pessimist")
Multus – many	*plus* – more	*plurimus* – most

ADVERBS

Stiff drink required for these.

Not much to them, but what there is, is pointlessly complicated. To form an adverb from an *-us, -a, -um* style adjective, like *dignus, -a, -um* – worthy or *tutus, -a, -um* – safe, swap *-e* or *-o* for the *-us*. There's no way of telling which to plump for, except from personal knowledge. So *dignus* (worthy) goes to *digne* (worthily), *tutus* (safe) to *tuto* (safely), and no one can explain why.

Useful adjectives are inevitably irregular, most strikingly: *bonus* – good goes to *bene* – well. Restaurant Italian – "*Tutto bene, Luigi. Il conto, per favore*" – should help here.

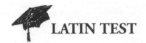

LATIN TEST

In February 2006, it was reported in the *Daily Telegraph* that Ista, a German hip hop band which raps in Latin, was re-forming after a sudden boom in popularity.

The band was formed a decade ago by seven bored classics pupils at a school in Wilhelmshaven. They roped in their teacher, Edgar Barwig, to make sure the lyrics were in good Latin.

The members of the band have now become architects, teachers, a nurse and parents, but they have got back together after their music came back into vogue.

"Over the years we have sold around 2,500 CDs," said one band member, Lars Janssen, "Between ten and twenty are bought per month from our internet site.

"But recently that has doubled and the media interest has been enormous. People have found us over the internet and we have sold CDs to people in the US and all across Europe. Latin is a good language to rap in actually. It has a good rhythm and can be to the point."

To mark their comeback, the band released a new song – *Caesaris Blues*, about being bored in Latin lessons. Their breakthrough track, though, was *Status Quo?* Here it is – see if you can translate it before looking at the translation.

Status Quo?

Radii solis per fenestras
Funduntur; utinam natem
Cum sodalibus, sed –
Hercle! Fallimur.

Nobis praeest blatero, qui
Semper dicat inepta, dum
Impleti simus eius summa
Amentia.

Sun rays stream through the window.
I wish I could go swimming with my friends but,
bloody Hell, we've messed up.

There's a blithering idiot in charge of us,
who keeps saying idiotic things
until we're sick to death of
his nonsense.

The Women's Institute War Cry, Verbal Abuse and The John Cleese Guide to Latin Lessons

Even the brightest people sometimes slip up on the minutiae (from *minutia, -ae, f.* – smallness) of Latin grammar. Just look at clever old John Cleese (Clifton Sports Academy, Downing College, Cambridge) when he played a Roman centurion in *The Life of Brian*:

> BRIAN *approaches the palace to graffiti the wall with an anti- Roman slogan. He begins writing, oblivious to the Roman patrol approaching from behind. The slogan reads "ROMANES EUNT DOMUS".*
> CENTURION: What's this, then? "ROMANES EUNT DOMUS"? "People called Romanes they go the house"?
> BRIAN: It says "Romans go home".
> CENTURION: No it doesn't. What's Latin for "Roman"?

BRIAN: (hesitates)

CENTURION: Come on, come on!

BRIAN: (uncertain) "ROMANUS."

CENTURION: Goes like?

BRIAN: "ANNUS"?

CENTURION: Vocative plural of "ANNUS" is?

BRIAN: "ANNI."

Centurion: (takes paintbrush from Brian and paints over) "RO-MA-NI". "EUNT"? What is "EUNT"?

BRIAN: "Go."

CENTURION: Conjugate the verb "to go"!

BRIAN: "IRE". "EO", "IS", "IT", "IMUS", "ITIS", "EUNT".

CENTURION: So "EUNT" is ...?

Brian: Third person plural present indicative, "They go."

CENTURION: But "Romans, go home!" is an order, so you must use the ...? (lifts Brian by his hairs)

BRIAN: The... imperative.

CENTURION: Which is?

BRIAN: Ahm, oh, oh, "I", "I"!

CENTURION: How many Romans? (pulls harder)

BRIAN: Plural, plural! "ITE."

CENTURION: (strikes over "EUNT" and paints "ITE" on the wall) (satisfied) "I-TE". "DOMUS"?

Nominative? "Go home", this is motion towards, isn't it, boy?

BRIAN: (very anxious) Dative?

CENTURION: (draws his sword and holds it to Brian's throat)

BRIAN: Ahh! No, ablative, ablative, sir. No, the, accusative, accusative, ah, DOMUM, sir.

CENTURION: Except that "DOMUS" takes the ...?

BRIAN:... the locative, sir!

CENTURION: Which is?

BRIAN: "DOMUM."

CENTURION: (satisfied) "DOMUM" (strikes out "DOMUS" and writes "DOMUM") "-MUM." Understand?

BRIAN: Yes sir.

CENTURION: Now write it down a hundred times.

BRIAN: Yes sir, thank you sir, hail Caesar, sir.

CENTURION: (salutes) Hail Caesar. If it's not done by sunrise, I'll cut your balls off.

Actually John Cleese's centurion wasn't quite right. Yes, *domus* behaves oddly, and yes, "*Romani, ite domum*" is right, but it isn't the locative that Brian used.

The locative is a strange, one-off case, used only when you're "at" or "in" a place. And the locative of *domus*, meaning "at home", is "*domi*". Here are the other rules for the locative:

First and Second Declension singular – use the genitive case.
Eg: *Romae* – in Rome, at Rome
Corinthi – in Corinth, at Corinth

Third Declension singular – use the dative.
Eg: *Carthagini* – at Carthage, in Carthage

First, Second and Third Declension plural – use the ablative.
Eg: *Athenis* – in Athens, at Athens
Sardibus – in Sardes, at Sardes

John Cleese's centurion was mixing up the locative of *domus* with a different rule. With *domus* and *casa (casa, -ae, f.* – house), the prepositions *ad, ab* and *in* are not used. The same goes for the names of cities (Rome, Athens, Sparta etc) and small islands (Sicily, Crete etc.). So,

1. Places "to which": name in the accusative without *ad*.
Eg. *Romam* – to Rome   *Carthaginem* – to Carthage
    Cretam – to Crete   *Domum* – home, as in Brian's
                                          "Romans, go home."

2. Places "from which": name in the ablative without *ab*.

Eg. *Brundisio* – from Brundisium

Athenis – from Athens

Sicilia – from Sicily

THE "DOS AND DON'TS" OF DOING WORDS – VERBS

Verbs are trickier than adjectives, and just as crucial.

Just to make things even more difficult, nouns *decline* and verbs *conjugate*. To make your head swim a bit more, there are five declensions and four conjugations. But just so you can get a feel for them now, the basic rule is that all verbs in the present tense roughly follow the endings of the most famous verb in Latin, *amo*.

Or, if you want a crude way of remembering a rough version of these endings that makes bored thirteen-year-old boys laugh even halfway through double Latin, remember the vulgarism from earlier – po, piss, pist, pimus, pistis, pants.

With this little vulgarism in mind, you should be able to spot whether any verb is 1st, 2nd or 3rd person; singular or plural.

Future and past tenses, which we'll also learn later on, have much the same endings with slightly different roots. I'm just giving you these little pointers on verbs before dealing with them in full, so we can start to do some sentences.

The Greatest Poem in the English Language

The only irregular verb you really need to know inside out is the verb "to be". It's hard to sugar the pill of learning, declining and conjugating nouns and verbs, particularly one as irregular as "to be". The closest thing to sugar I can find is some old telly footage of a drunk Richard Burton, squeezed into a far too tight red polo-neck, spending his declining years conjugating his favourite verb.

"The greatest poem in the English language," he said, "is the verb 'to be'. I AM [long pause], you ARE [longer pause], he, she or it IS, we ARE, you ARE, they ARE."

I think his point was that this rote conjugation had a sort of beauty to it, as an affirmation of life. Either way, you can con yourself into thinking the same about Latin conjugation in general and there certainly is a poetry to conjugating if you do it quickly enough. Try saying, "*Sum, es, est, sumus, estis, sunt*" as quickly as possible and it begins to stick in your mind as a little poem to be enjoyed rather than a list to be learnt.

You may recall the phrase, "*Civis Romanus sum*" ("I am a Roman citizen"), which became famous in 1850 when Lord Palmerston sent British ships to Athens to settle the claims of Don Pacifico, a Jew from Gibraltar and a British subject, whose house had been damaged by the Greeks.

Palmerston said at the time, "As the Roman, in days of old, held himself free from indignity when he could say, '*Civis Romanus Sum*,' so also a British subject in whatever land he may be, shall feel confident that the watchful eye and the strong arm of England will protect him against injustice and wrong."

Apart from the verb "to be", you needn't learn the irregular verbs and nouns yet. The simple principle to remember is the one we've already come across: THE MORE REGULARLY USED, THE MORE IRREGULARLY SPELT. This is because, so experts think, the more familiar words have been warped by over-use.

Your First Sentence

Paulus Gasconius uxorem suam Sherylam percussit.
Paul Gascoigne beat his wife Sheryl.

Sheryla Gasconia Paulum virum suum deseruit.
Sheryl Gascoigne left her husband Paul.

uxor, -oris, f. – a wife

percutio, -ere, percussi, percussum – I strike hard (thus "percussion")

desero, -ere, -ui, desertum – I desert

suus, -a, -um, adj. – his, her, their own

vir, viri, m. – a man, husband

Gazza lacrimans

Now to deal properly with verbs. Deep breath time again. As I said, there are four conjugations of verbs. The way to sum up a verb is in its so-called principal parts, that is, the four familiar forms of each verb.

So, with *amo*, the principal parts are: *amo, amare, amavi, amatum* "I love", "to love", "I have loved", and the so-called supine, which means "having been loved".

Thus in any latin dictionary, the principal parts of a verb are laid out next to its definition, to show the four basic forms that you'll come across: i.e. *facio, facere, feci, factum* – "I do/make."

The first principal part is the most simple form of the verb, the first person (that is "I...") singular present. This always ends in *-o: exsudo* – "I sweat", "exude"*; turpo* – "I make ugly", "defile."

Incidentally, a good way to remember the spelling of the adjective, principal, (as opposed to the noun, principle), is the fact that the Latin adjective – meaning "leading", from *princeps, -ipis m.* – prince, is *principalis, -e.* (By the way, when I list only two genders, like here with *principalis, -e,* that's because it goes the same in both the masculine and the feminine).

The second principal part is the infinitive (i.e. "to stroke", "to fiddle" etc.). This always ends with *-re,* but the letter before the *-re* changes according to the conjugation.

---

amo, **amare** – **to love** (first conjugation)
moneo, **monere** – **to warn** (second conjugation)
rego, **regere** – **to rule** (third conjugation)
audio, **audire** – **to hear** (fourth conjugation)

You can use the infinitive as a noun, and the noun is always neuter. So, *Errare est humanum, ignosci divinum* – "To err is human, to forgive divine" (Alexander Pope).

English pedants date their dislike of a split infinitive from Latin. Since you can't split a Latin infinitive, because it's a single word, you shouldn't do it in English, or so the pedants say.

That seems bloody stupid to me – Latin and English are two different languages.

"To boldly go where no man has gone before" (Captain Kirk, *Starship Enterprise Logbook*) actually sounds better than "Boldly to go…" or "To go boldly…", and is easily translated into Latin – "*Ire audacter eo quo nemo antea.*"

You can also use the infinitive to express desire.

"He wanted to buy Sienna Miller a chariot."

"*Cariam Siennae* [buy a chariot for Sienna – dative of Sienna, Siennae] *Millae emere voluit.*"

VOCAB.

emo, emere, emi, emptum – I buy (as in pre-emptive strike, and "*caveat emptor*" – Let the buyer beware).

The principal parts of *eo* – to go, by the way, are a nightmare: *eo, ire, ii, itum.* Incidentally, the English 'ire' has nothing to do with *ire* – to go, and everything to do with *ira, irae f.* – anger.

To form the perfect infinitive, you take the perfect stem –
say *lacrimavi* – I have cried – and add on *-sse* at the end:

Better to have loved and lost than never to have loved
at all.
Amavisse et amisisse mallem quam omnino non amavisse.

VOCAB.
amitto, -mittere, -misi, -missum – I lose
malo, malle, malui – I wish
omnino – altogether

The third principal part is the perfect tense:

> *amo, amare, **amavi***
> *moneo, monere, **monui***
> *rego, regere, **rexi***
> *audio, audire, **audivi***

And the fourth principal part is the supine, which doesn't
have an English equivalent. It is formed from the perfect
participle of the verb in its nominative, neuter form.

The supine is a wonderfully useful little device, because it
converts the verb into an adjective – *amatus* (beloved),
lacrimatus (wept over), *necatus* (murdered), *fatigatus* (tired).

This is known as the past participle, as you'll see later.

> *Cynthia prima suis miserum me cepit ocellis,*
> *contactum nullis ante cupidinibus.*

Cynthia first trapped me with her little eyes, miserable old me who hadn't been touched [*contactum* – past participle] by desire before.

Propertius, Elegies I, Cynthia

VOCAB.

capio, capere, cepi, captum – I capture
ocellus, -i m. – a little eye (diminutive of *oculus, -i, m.* – eye)
contingo, contingere, contigi, contactum – I touch
cupido, -idinis, f. – desire (as in Cupid)

So it always ends in *-um* and has mildly differing forms in the different conjugations:

> *amo, amare, amavi,* ***amatum***
> *moneo, monere, monui,* ***monitum***
> *rego, regere, rexi,* ***rectum***
> *audio, audire, audivi,* ***auditum***

Note too that the supine is the fertile source for English-related words: amatory, monitor, auditory…

Arnold Schwarzenegger was wrongly christened the Governator when he became the Governor of California in 2003. He should have been called the Gubernator, the Roman for governor, the man who would govern a province. It comes from *guberno, -are, -avi, -atum*. In the same way, The Terminator comes from *termino, -are, -avi, -atum* – I end.

There's no need to learn all the conjugations off by heart, yet, but just be aware that there are four of them and that they all have slightly different roots. Just for completeness's sake, though, here are all the four present tenses of the four conjugations:

1. *amo – I love*
   amas – you (s.) love
   amat – he/she/it loves
   amamus – we love
   amatis – you (pl.) love
   amant – they love

2. *moneo – I warn*
   mones – you (s.) warn
   monet – he/she/it warns
   monemus – we warn
   monetis – you (pl.) warn
   monent – they warn

3. *rego – I rule*
   regis – you (s.) rule
   regit – he/she/it rules
   regimus – we rule
   regitis – you (pl.) rule
   regunt – they rule

4. *audio – I hear*
   audis – you (s.) hear
   audit – he/she/it hears
   audimus – we hear
   auditis – you (pl.) hear
   audiunt – they hear

For the hundreds of years that Latin has been taught in English schools, "*Amo, amas, amat…*" has been the subject's iconic cry – thus the title of this book. As the basis for learning the simplest form of verb and one of the most crucial – "I love" – it still holds that iconic power.

Eugenie Howard-Johnston, a 25-year-old graduate of Cheltenham Ladies' College and New College, Oxford, with a fetching line in scrunched-up hair and boho jangly jewellery meets Dad's V-neck, teaches Latin at St Saviour's and St Olave's, a comprehensive in Elephant and Castle in London.

Miss Howard-Johnston – or Miss Ho-Jo, as her pupils like to call her – teaches Latin by rapping in the language and surprisingly good it is, too. (And there, buried away two thirds through the rap, is the old cry heard through the grandest schools in the land for centuries – *amo, amas, amat…*):

In urbano jungle of SE1
Leo lays aside suum gun,
Walks on stage portans his Latin book,
Turns to page unam, has a brief look,
Shuts id iterum, begins to clap,
Stamps his pedes et starts his rap:
"Odi et amo – that's how it goes
A hater and a lover and I guess it shows:
Ego everyday in urbe fight

Tum turn to find some amorem at night.
Cur tu stand there looking so yellow?
Num tu afraid that ego bellum gero?
No! Pacem quaero – and yeah it's cheesy
Sed tibi dico, that it ain't easy."
He turns around and ridet at his mum,
She smiles back while the canes hum.
"Amo, amas, amat," they whisper in time
As Leo continues with his rhyme.
"Amamus, amatis and amant,"
The canes sing as the descant.
The lights go down, the cives applaud –
"Leo!" clamant, "tu es noster Latin Lord!"

PRONOUNS

Pronouns are tricky, fiddly things to learn, partly because they all sound so similar – *is, ea, id, ipse, ille* etc – but they're pretty crucial.

Me, Me, Me

An unsurprisingly well-used word in Latin is "me" or more correctly "I" – or *ego*", as it is in Latin. This goes:

	Singular	Plural
NOM	*Ego*	*Nos*
ACC	*Me*	*Nos*
GEN	*Mei*	*Nostri/Nostrum*
DAT	*Mihi*	*Nobis*
ABL	*Me*	*Nobis*

Incidentally, a "nostrum" is a medicine or a scheme promising all sorts of cures, with no demonstrable value. In one of the examples of how a derivation can get unrecognisably warped from its original meaning, the word comes from the cry of the medicine-seller, "*Nostrum, nostrum*" – "Ours, ours (…come get our quack remedy, answer to the crisis in the Middle East, secret of true love *etc*).

You, *tu*, goes:

	Singular	Plural
NOM	*Tu*	*Vos*
ACC	*Te*	*Vos*
GEN	*Tui*	*Vestri/Vestrum*
DAT	*Tibi*	*Vobis*
ABL	*Te*	*Vobis*

Being Self-ish

While, in English, we have the nice, lazy device of adding on "self" to a pronoun to add emphasis and make what is called a reflexive pronoun, the Romans had different words for each self.

"Himself", "herself" or "itself" are all translated into *se*, as in *per se* ("in and of itself").

Helpfully, there is no plural form for *se* – i.e. you use *se* to mean themselves as well as himself/itself/herself. And there is no nominative of *se*, because, as it were, somebody can only do something to himself as an object.

There is no separate word for "myself"; it is covered by *ego*, as above – *me*.

ACC	*Se*	– himself, herself, itself or themselves
GEN	*Sui*	– of himself
DAT	*Sibi*	– to himself
ABL	*Se*	– by, with or from himself.

THE FUTURE TENSE

To put it simply, first and second conjugation verbs like *amo* and *moneo* throw in a '*b*' for the future; third and fourth ones like *rego* and *audio* throw in an '*e*' in their roots:

1. *amabo – I will love*
   amabis – you (s.) will love
   amabit – he/she/it will love
   amabimus – we will love
   amabitis – you (pl.) will love
   amabunt – they will love

2. *monebo – I will warn*
   monebis – you (s.) will warn
   monebit – he/she/it will warn
   monebimus – we will warn
   monebitis – you (pl.) will warn
   monebunt – they will warn

3. *regam – I will rule*
   reges – you (s.) will rule
   reget – he/she/it will rule
   regemus – we will rule
   regetis – you (pl.) will rule
   regent – they will rule

4. *audiam – I will hear*
   audies - you (s.) will hear
   audiet - he/she/it will hear
   audiemus – we will hear
   audietis – you (pl.) will hear
   audient – they will hear

THE IMPERFECT TENSE

This means the tense, "I was tittering/weeping/raking". It's an easy one to do because it's much the same through the conjugations. All you have to do is add on *-bam* at the end of each verb and then conjugate pretty much as normal.

1. *amabam – I was loving*
   amabas – you (s.) were loving
   amabat – he/she/it was loving
   amabamus – we were loving
   amabatis – you (pl.) were loving
   amabant – they were loving

2. *monebam – I was warning*
   monebas – you (s.) were warning
   monebat – he/she/it was warning
   monebamus – we were warning
   monebatis – you (pl.) were warning
   monebant – they were warning

3. *regebam – I was ruling*
   regebas – you (s.) were ruling
   regebat – he/she/it was ruling
   regebamus – we were ruling
   regebatis – you (pl.) were ruling
   regebant – they were ruling

4. *audiebam* – *I was hearing*
   audiebas – *you (s.) were hearing*
   audiebat – *he/she/it was hearing*
   audiebamus – *we were hearing*
   audiebatis – *you (pl.) were hearing*
   audiebant – *they were hearing*

THE PERFECT TENSE

The best-known three perfect tenses in Latin are the ones on the top of Caesar's CV (short for "curriculum vitae", literally "the running order of life"; curriculum comes from *curro, currere, cucurri, cursum* – I run): *Veni, vidi, vici* – "I came, I saw, I conquered" (as Caesar said when he defeated Pharnaces, King of Pontus, in one day at the Battle of Zela in 47 BC).

Actually, the perfect is wrongly named. It's certainly not perfectly easy to learn or perfectly formed.

But then our use of the word perfect is different to the original Latin use of the word. The word "perfect" comes from *perficio, perficere, perfeci, perfectum* – "I do thoroughly". So *perfectus* means "having been done thoroughly".

This is as opposed to the imperfect, which means an ongoing act in the past that hasn't been completed: i.e.

imperfect – "I was kissing her, when her enormous brother Sid turned up"; perfect – "I kissed her, and then told her that I was more attracted to her enormous brother Sid."

There are two ways of translating the perfect: "I broiled" or "I have broiled".

The second sense must be relied upon for the cleverest show-off joke in the history of the British Empire, made by Sir Charles Napier, the nineteenth-century general whose statue in Trafalgar Square Ken Livingstone took against so vehemently in October 2000.

Charged with fighting for and occupying the Indian city of Miani in the province of Sind in north-west India in 1843, Sir Charles pulled it off nice and quickly. His telegram back to the Indian Office was nice and quick, too. "Peccavi" is all he wrote, i.e. "I have sinned," from *pecco, peccare, peccavi, peccatum* – "I sin". Geddit?

Anyway, the joke depends on some clever classicist being around in the Indian Office on the day the telegram arrived; a classicist so clever that he knew to translate it as "I have sinned" as opposed to "I sinned", which wouldn't have made much sense to Lord Palmerston in Downing Street at the time.

The perfect tense has all sorts of irregular endings, varies greatly across the conjugations and is the point where verbs have a sort of nervous breakdown and go into meltdown. That melted-down form is, annoyingly, where some of the related nouns are drawn from. So *rego* – I rule, goes *rego, regere, rexi, rectum*. Because the noun comes from the perfect, the Latin for "ruler" or "king" is then not "reg", but "rex". So here are the four conjugations.

1. *amavi – I have loved*
   amavisti – you (s.) have loved
   amavit – he/she/it has loved
   amavimus – we have loved
   amavistis – you have loved
   amaverunt – they have loved

2. *monui – I have warned*
   monuisti – you (s.) have warned
   monuit – he/she/it has warned
   monuimus – we have warned
   monuistis – you (pl.) have warned
   monuerunt – they have warned

3. *rexi – I have ruled*
   rexisti – you (s.) have ruled
   rexit – he/she/it has ruled
   reximus – we have ruled
   rexistis – you (pl.) have ruled
   rexerunt – they have ruled

4. *audivi – I have heard*
   audivisti – you (s.) have heard
   audivit – he/she/it has heard
   audivimus – we have heard
   audivistis – you (pl.) have heard
   audiverunt – they have heard

THE PLUPERFECT TENSE

The pluperfect – literally plusperfect – means "more perfect" or, if you like, "even more completed" i.e. further back in time. So you translate the pluperfect – "I had snuffled/ snogged/ smooched."

Some consolation of going through all the rigmarole of learning the perfect means that the pluperfect becomes a cinch. All you do is take the perfect root above, and add in:

-eram

-eras

-erat

-eramus

-eratis

-erant

So the four conjugations go:

1. *amaveram – I had loved*
    amaveras – you (s.) had loved
    amaverat – he/she/it had loved
    amaveramus – we had loved
    amaveratis – you (pl.) had loved
    amaverant – they had loved

2. *monueram – I had warned*
    monueras – you (s.) had warned
    monuerat – he/she/it had warned
    monueramus – we had warned
    monueratis – you (pl.) had warned
    monuerant – they had warned

3. *rexeram – I had ruled*
    rexeras – you (s.) had ruled
    rexerat – he/she/it had ruled
    rexeramus – we had ruled
    rexeratis – you (pl.) had ruled
    rexerant – they had ruled

4. *audiveram – I had heard*
   audiveras – you (s.) had heard
   audiverat – he/she/it had heard
   audiveramus – we had heard
   audiveratis – you (pl.) had heard
   audiverant – they had heard

ORDERING SOMEONE ABOUT – THE IMPERATIVE

When you tell someone to do something directly – "Wash
your mouth out with Harpic", "Bury him before *rigor mortis*
('the stiffness of death', by the way) sets in" – you use the
imperative.

Although in English we only use one sort of imperative,
whether we're telling a six-month-old baby to go to sleep or,
over a PA, telling 60,000 Arsenal fans not to drink on the terraces, the Romans had a singular and a plural imperative.

The comforting thing, though, is that the imperative is very
simple and, fittingly, curt. For the singular imperative for *amo*
moneo, and *audio,* all you do is take the root, *ama, mone,* and
audi (like the car) – and that's it. So "Love her" is "*Ama eam*".
"Show the picture" is "*Monstra imaginem*".

The plural is easy, too – just add *-te* on to the singular:

Tell Laura I love her (addressed to one person).

Narra Laurae me eam amare.

Tell Laura I love her (addressed to more than one person).

Narrate Laurae me eam amare.

Rego is predictably difficult, going *rege* in the singular, but *regite* in the plural. A famous Second Declension imperative is "*Cave canem*" – "Beware of the dog."

Cave canem – Postmen of Pompeii, you have been warned

PARTICIPLES

Participles are what you make when you turn a noun into an adjective, i.e. "the 'running' boy", "the 'kissing' gate", "the 'mass-murdering' grandmother". In the present tense, they're formed by adding on *-ans, -ens* or whatever the root might be to the verb. So the classic conjugations are *amans, monens,* *regens, audiens.* They all decline like Third Declension adjectives:

	Singular	Plural
NOM.	*amans*	*amantes*
VOC.	*amans*	*amantes*
ACC.	*amantem*	*amantes*
GEN.	*amantis*	*amantium*
DAT.	*amanti*	*amantibus*
ABL.	*amanti*	*amantibus*

The present participle of amo

There's a perfect participle, too, which is, roughly, formed by adding on *-tus* to the verb's root. This, in the neuter, is the supine – the last principal part of the verb, which we met earlier: *amatum, monitum, rectum, auditum.*

So... *amatus, monitus, rectus, auditus* – "having been loved", "having been advised", "having been ruled", "having been heard" – all decline like *dominus* in the masculine, *mensa* in the feminine and *bellum* in the neuter:

> *amatus, -a, -um*
> *monitus, -a, -um*
> *rectus, -a, -um*
> *auditus, -a, -um*

There is also a very odd-looking future participle. This is made by taking the perfect participle stem, *amat-, monit-* etc, and adding on *-urus, -ura, -urum,* depending on the case:

> *amaturus, -a, -um*
> *moniturus, -a, -um*
> *recturus, -a, -um*
> *auditurus, -a, -um*

The future participle is a marvellously versatile, compact thing. It can mean, "about to do…", "on the verge of doing…", "just before doing…" For e.g.,

Gordonus Brownus, Antonium Blaerum victurus, se pharmaca potentissima cotidie consumere admisit.

Just when he was about to beat Tony Blair [from *vinco, vincere, vici, victum* – I conquer], Gordon Brown admitted to a severe Class-A drug habit.

BOTANISTS' LATIN

If you're short of laughs, take a walk round a National Trust garden this afternoon, and look for the Women's Institute

Walk. You'll know what I mean when you see it: a group of women in middle-to-late-middle age, walking as slowly as possible without actually stopping.

And then they do stop, as they pass an obscure-looking plant. Gently pointing at the plant, they start to make a very particular tribal cry, distinguished by a series of tentative questions, disguising huge confidence and great doses of one-upmanship. And a lot of Latin.

"What sort of foxglove is that?"

"*Scrophulariaceae.*"

"Yes, I know that. But what's the species?"

"*Digitalis.*"

"Yes, but what sort?"

"*Digitalis lutea,* isn't it?"

"Isn't that the yellow one?"

"Of course it is. Silly me. That's *digitalis purpurea.* They're all over the hedgerows on the Carmarthen road to Llandovery."

To get over this showing-off, you may be tempted to go to the nearest National Trust café and drink as much Audley End Elderflower Wine or Waddesdon Home Brew as they've got in stock.

Or you might want to learn how to do the WI Walk and War Cry yourself. It's actually very easy and it makes a lot of sense.

Different countries and different regions of each country develop different words for the same plant: a Scottish bluebell is a harebell in England and Wales. So it's logical to have a common name for each plant, and, given the shared Latin root to most European languages, it's logical that the name is in Latin.

A Guatemalan botanist will no doubt stare off, nonplussed, in the direction of the Andes if you start talking about daffodils. Say Narcissus and you'll have his undivided attention.

Plants with lots of features in common can be divided up into species, genus and family. The *species* (the plural, nice and confusingly, is also *species*) are the tightest little groups, normally found in the same area. They don't tend to interbreed, although they can; witness the victory of the coarse Spanish bluebell over the delicate English one.

If the species have enough characteristics in common, they are grouped together into a *genus* (plural, *genera*). And *genera* with features in common are called families, like orchids or bamboo.

So, in the WI War Cry above, *Scrophulariaceae* is the plant family name. *Digitalis*, meaning foxglove, is the *genus* name. And *Digitalis lutea* (yellow foxglove) or *Digitalis purpurea* (purple foxglove) is the species name.

Here are some words used to classify different species:

nigrum – black, *alba* – white, *gigantium* – large, *cespitosa* – tufted, *foetidissima* – horrible smelling, *maritime* – found by the sea, *Cambricum* – Welsh, *Canadensis* – natural to Canada, *officinale* – medicinal.

To get an A in the WI War Cry, you can learn the even more precise classifications. The prefix "ssp." before the species name means "*subspecies*", i.e. another group within the species group.

If the species name has "*var.*"(short for "variety") in front of it, that means the plant is a naturally occurring mutation that a gardener has deliberately propagated.

If the Latin name has an English proper name or a descriptive name after it, say *Daphne bholua* "*Zeta Jones*" or *Rosa azura* "*Blues in the Night*", then it's a garden cultivar. That means it's a plant that's been cultivated for colour, smell or foliage, and given a special name by its cultivator to sum up its special quality or to show the cultivator's reverence for his favourite B-list actress from Swansea.

Incidentally, much the same system applies to animals, as Jeeves points out to Bertie Wooster in *Right Ho, Jeeves* (1934):

> "You must have heard of newts. Those little sort of lizard things that charge around in ponds."
>
> "Oh, yes, sir. The aquatic members of the family Salamandridae which constitute the species Molge."

ACTIVE AND PASSIVE

These words may sound scary, but they're simple enough.

An active verb is exactly that – it means acting, *doing* something to somebody else. A passive verb means exactly that – i.e. doing nothing and having something done to oneself. So if you are "being thwacked", "are about to be flogged" or "have been bullied", then you're in the passive.

A rough rule of thumb is to look for an *-r* at the end of a verb if you're on the lookout for a passive. Here's how they go:

> 1. *amor – I am loved*
>   *amaris – you (s.) are loved*
>   *amatur – he/she/it is loved*
>   *amamur – we are loved*
>   *amamini – you (pl.) are loved*
>   *amantur – they are loved*
>
>
> 2. *moneor – I am warned*
>   *moneris – you (s.) are warned*
>   *monetur – he/she/it is warned*
>   *monemur – we are warned*
>   *monemini – you (pl.) are warned*
>   *monentur – they are warned*

3. *regor – I am ruled*
   regeris – you (s.) are ruled
   regitur – he/she/it is ruled
   regimur – we are ruled
   regimini – you (pl.) are ruled
   reguntur – they are ruled

4. *audior – I am heard*
   audiris – you (s.) are heard
   auditur – he/she/it is heard
   audimur – we are heard
   audimini – you (pl.) are heard
   audiuntur – they are heard

DEPONENT

An annoying little wrinkle on the passive is that some verbs that decline like passive verbs turn out to be active.

These are called deponent verbs and their futures, imperfects, perfects etc. all go like future passives, imperfect passives etc.. Even more annoyingly, they're quite common. Among the ones you'll regularly bump into are:

Hortor, hortari, hortatus sum – I encourage

Loquor, loqui, locutus sum – I speak (thus "eloquent", "loquacious")

Reor, reri, ratus sum – I think (thus "rational")

Sequor, sequi, secutus sum – I follow (thus "sequence")

Nascor, nasci, natus sum – I am born (thus "pre/ postnatal")

Patior, pati, passus sum – I suffer (thus the "passive" voice, as opposed to the "active" voice, which comes from *ago, agere, egi, actum* – "I do").

One of the useful things about the deponent is that its past participle is active – i.e. it can take an object – not passive, like other verbs. That means you can use the deponent past participle in a much freer way than the passive past participles: "Having suffered life, he loved death," is just "*Vitam passus, mortem amavit.*"

But, if you wanted to say, "Once he'd made his bed and brushed his teeth, he killed himself," you'd have to make everything clumsier by turning each little clause into an ablative absolute – "The bed having been made, the teeth having been brushed…": *Lecto formato, dentibus versatis, se occidit.*

VOCAB.

lectus, -i m. – bed

formo, -are – I form, shape
dens, dentis m. – a tooth
verro, verrere, verri, versum – I brush, scour
occido, -ere, occidi, occisum – I kill

THE ABLATIVE ABSOLUTE

If the words "ablative absolute" send the spirits plunging, better to think of it as the "while" word. In other words, if you think of an expression with two things going on at the same time, the "while" bit is an ablative absolute.

Suave, mari magno turbantibus aequora ventis,
E terra magnum alterius spectare laborem.

How lovely it is to gaze from the shore at somebody having a terrible time, while the wind whips up the waters on the huge sea.

Lucretius, *On the Nature of Things*,
The Epicurean Ideal – Peace of Mind

For an ablative absolute, you put the both the noun in the ablative, and the verb in the ablative of the participle form. "*Te dormiente…*" "With you sleeping…"

However you need to be on your guard when translating ablative absolutes. It is most important to try and steer clear of "with the legionary bearing malice to the ditches, the Gaul assaulted him" school of heavy-handed Latin.

FUTURE PASSIVE

The future passive is a funny little hybrid of the future active with similar endings to the present passive. A bit of a nightmare to learn.

>   1. *amabor – I will be loved*
>   *amaberis – you(s.) will be loved*
>   *amabitur – he/she/it will be loved*
>   *amabimur – we will be loved*
>   *amabimini – you (pl.) will be loved*
>   *amabuntur – they will be loved*
>
>   2. *monebor – I will be warned*
>   *moneberis – you (s.) will be warned*
>   *monebitur – he/she/it will be warned*
>   *monebimur – we will be warned*
>   *monebimini – you (pl.) will be warned*
>   *monebuntur – they will be warned*

3. *regar – I will be ruled*
   regeris – you(s.) will be ruled
   regetur – he/she/it will be ruled
   regemur – we will be ruled
   regemini – you (pl.) will be ruled
   regentur – they will be ruled

4. *audiar – I will be heard*
   audieris – you(s.) will be heard
   audietur – he/she/it will be heard
   audiemur – we will be heard
   audiemini – you (pl.) will be heard
   audientur – they will be heard

PERFECT PASSIVE

The perfect passive is easy as you like. All you do is take the perfect participle and add on the verb "to be" at the end. So "I have been loved/shown/ruled/heard" goes:

Amatus/monitus/rectus/auditus ...	*sum*
	es
	est
	sumus
	estis
	sunt

1484 YEARS OF PURPLE TOGAS – OR ROMAN
EMPERORS AND THEIR GREATEST HITS

Phew. That was quite heavy going, so I think it's time for a brief digression on Roman emperors. There's no need to learn them all, though. There are far too many of them who did nothing of interest. But here's a list of the notable ones – with important juicy facts added where needed.

Augustus was the first Roman emperor, because he invented the job in 31 BC after centuries of the Roman Republic, which had lasted ever since the expulsion from Rome of the last Tarquinian king, Tarquinius Superbus, in 510 BC.

Before Augustus made himself emperor, there had been two triumvirates (from *tres* and *viri* – three men) in charge: 60-54 BC – Caesar, Pompey and Crassus; 43–33 BC – Octavian (as Augustus was originally called), Lepidus and Mark Antony.

Augustus took up the surname Caesar in honour of Julius, his great-uncle. All Augustus's successors then took on the name Caesar, too, accruing the same sort of Brownie points that the royal family got by ditching the surname Saxe-Coburg-Gotha and assuming "Windsor" instead.

The Germans and the Russians also took on the name Caesar in later centuries in the form of Kaisers and Tsars.

You might be interested to know that Julius Caesar had been offered the role of emperor but turned it down three times. He was happy enough wearing purple and being dictator four times, and being deified in 42 BC, two years after he was murdered by Brutus and Cassius. (Emperors took to wearing purple, partly because it was such a difficult dye to get hold of – it cost more, ounce for ounce, than gold. 10,000 Murex molluscs had to be crushed to produce enough dye for one "toga picta" – painted toga.)

Anyway, here goes:

31 BC-14 AD: Augustus – He ended a century of civil war in Rome and, as he said in his show-off autobiography, *Res Gestae* – The Things I've Done (literally, "The Things Done") – "I found Rome a city of brick and made it marble."

The month of August (Latin *Augustus*) is named after Augustus; before it had been called *Sextilis* (the sixth month of the Roman calendar). August has 31 days because Augustus wanted his month to be as long as Julius Caesar's July.

Augustus set in place the so-called *Pax Romana* for the next

200 years (notwithstanding minor scraps with the British and half of Europe). He began the expansion of the empire, which over the next two centuries saw it spread its boundaries to Armenia, Mesopotamia, the Arabian desert, the Red Sea, Nubia, the Sahara, the Moroccan mountains, the Atlantic Ocean, the Irish Sea, Scotland, the North Sea, the Rhine, the Danube, the Black Sea, and the Caucasus.

***

14 AD-37 AD: Tiberius – Augustus's stepson, who spent the last decade of his life in his clifftop palace in Capri, occasionally hurling enemies into the sea.

Made the mistake of getting too pally with a minion, Sejanus, head of the elite, and presumably crack, Praetorian Guard. Sejanus, when in Tiberius's favour, assumed semi-imperial powers. Once he was out of the emperor's favour, the Praetorian Guard turned on Sejanus and executed him.

***

37-41 AD: Gaius (Caligula) – Neither quite as wet as John Hurt's portrayal of him in *I, Claudius*, nor as sexually depraved as Malcolm McDowell is in Gore Vidal's 1979 film, *Caligula*.

Certainly spoilt, possibly mad: got so close to his favourite racehorse, Incitatus, that he invited guests to dinner in Incitatus's name, and even considered making Incitatus a consul.

Caligula means "Little Boot", derived from his childhood in a Roman army camp, where he wore a miniature soldier's costume.

***

41-54 AD: Claudius – As in "I", the stuttering emperor played by Derek Jacobi in the 1977 series.

Certainly scholarly as depicted in the series, he also had a cruel streak, with an addiction to watching gladiators kill each other. Liked to watch his defeated opponents being executed.

But, on the plus side, Claudius did lead the second invasion of Britain in 43 AD, after Julius Caesar's first go (see Roman Britain, *infra*). Good old Claudius was so keen on us that he even called his son Britannicus, born in 41 AD, i.e. before the invasion.

Sadly, though, Claudius wasn't so keen on the boy and we missed out on the pleasure of an Emperor Britannicus. Instead the purple toga went to Claudius's adopted son, Nero.

***

54-68 AD: Nero – Not quite true that he fiddled while Roman burned. Certainly he had artistic leanings – although he was vigorously heterosexual, with two wives, Octavia and Poppaea – and took to appearing on stage and singing in public.

When a huge fire left most of Rome in ashes in 64 AD he did little to help rebuild the city and some suspected he lit the fires himself.

Nero did, though, build himself an elaborate, beautifully frescoed palace, the *Domus Aurea,* or Golden House. This selfishness, combined with his taste for singing, stoked the fiddling myth.

***

There were then various non-entities:

68-69 AD: Galba

69 AD: Otho

69 AD: Vitellius

69-79 AD: Vespasian, who began building the Colosseum

79-81 AD: Titus, who finished building it

81-96 AD: Domitian

96-98 AD: Nerva

Until:

98-117 AD: Trajan – Perhaps the greatest show-off of them all, with the erection of Trajan's Column recording his triumph over the Dacians of modern Romania in 101-102 and 105-106 AD.

On the friezes that wrap their way all around the column in the middle of Trajan's forum in Rome, the emperor is always shown as taller than other Romans, and much taller than the Dacians.

***

117-138 AD: Hadrian – As in the wall, 73 and a half miles long, six foot high, eight foot thick, stretching from Wallsend on the Tyne to Bowness at the head of Solway Firth.

***

138-161 AD: Antoninus Pius – Who, with his successor, Antoninus Pius set up the so-called Golden Age of the Roman Empire, the calm before the storm.

***

161-180 AD: Marcus Aurelius – The cleverest of the Roman emperors, whose *Meditations* are still in print.

Very avant-garde: "You will give yourself relief, if you do

every act of your life as if it were the last, laying aside all carelessness and passionate aversion from the commands of reason, and all hypocrisy, and self-love, and discontent with the portion which has been given to you" (*Meditations* II.V).

***

180-192 AD: Commodus – According to Edward Gibbon in *The History of the Decline and Fall of the Roman Empire*, "If a man were called to fix the period in the history of the world, during which the condition of the human race was most happy and prosperous, he would, without hesitation, name that which elapsed from the death of Domitian to the accession of Commodus."

With Commodus came the decline of the Roman Empire as the Praetorian Guard started to muscle in on the emperors' act.

***

Between 192 AD and 306 AD there are plenty of Emperors, but none that you will need to bother your head about, although if you want to show off, you could drop a Diadumenianus or an Elagabalus into conversation.

306-337 AD: Constantine I – Changed the world by converting to Christianity on his deathbed. This epoch-making decision grew out of the victory over Maxentius at the Battle of Milvian Bridge, outside Rome, in 312 AD.

The night before battle, Constantine saw the two Greek letters, Chi and Rho, the symbol of Christ, shining above the sun. He had his soldiers paint the symbol on their shields and, following his victory, he started considering his conversion.

He then went on to transfer the capital of the Roman Empire from Rome to the ancient city of Byzantium, renamed Constantinople, later to become Istanbul. Thus the 1953 hit by The Four Lads, *Istanbul (Not Constantinople),* which goes:

Istanbul was Constantinople.
Now it's Istanbul, not Constantinople.
Been a long time gone, Constantinople.
Now it's Turkish delight on a moonlit night.

Every gal in Constantinople
Lives in Istanbul, not Constantinople.
So if you've a date in Constantinople
She'll be waiting in Istanbul.

Even old New York was once New Amsterdam.
Why they changed it I can't say.

People just liked it better that way.
So take me back to Constantinople.

No, you can't go back to Constantinople.
Been a long time gone, Constantinople.
Why did Constantinople get the works?
That's nobody's business but the Turks.

Then we pass through various dynasties and partitions of empires until we come to:

1449-1453 AD: Constantine XI – The last Byzantine Emperor, indeed the last Roman Emperor, whose loss of Constantinople to Mehmet II in 1453 brought the whole shooting match to a close.

THANK JUPITER BOADICEA LOST
– THE JOYS OF ROMAN BRITAIN

Plumbing, central heating, Scotland, Wales, Christianity, the layout of our major cities…

All of these things emerged in Britain thanks to the two invasions of Britain by Claudius (43 AD) and Julius Caesar (although strictly speaking, he had two gos, in 55 and 54 BC).

And the other thing is Latin, of course. The invasions are why English is so full of Latinate words (around 65 per cent of the total), why British schoolboys started learning Latin obsessively in the Middle Ages, why some of them are still learning it obsessively, and why this book is coming out.

The best writer about Roman Britain was the great historian Tacitus. His prose isn't easy, but it is certainly clear and a fine model. You can use the following passages either to test your Latin or just to get close to an eye-witness view of Roman Britain. Tacitus wasn't actually ever in the country, but his father-in-law, Agricola, was governor of Britain.

In his account of the man, simply called *Agricola,* he describes Boadicea's revolt (or Boudicca, if you want to call her what she called herself, before later historians started playing around with her name).

When Claudius ordered the invasion of Britain in AD 43, the main target was Camulodunum (Colchester), the fortified Iron Age settlement of the Catuvellauni which had been ruled, until his death a few years before, by Cunobelinus (or Cymbeline, as in the Shakespeare play). Here is Tacitus in chapters 11 and 12 of the first book of his *Agricola:*

11. *Ceterum Britanniam qui mortales initio coluerint, indigenae an advecti, ut inter barbaros, parum compertum.*

Habitus corporum varii atque ex eo argumenta. Namque rutilae Caledoniam habitantium comae, magni artus Germanicam originem adseverant; Silurum colorati vultus, torti plerumque crines et posita contra Hispania Hiberos veteres traiecisse easque sedes occupasse fidem faciunt; proximi Gallis et similes sunt, seu durante originis vi, seu procurrentibus in diversa terris positio caeli corporibus habitum dedit.

In universum tamen aestimanti Gallos vicinam insulam occupasse credibile est. Eorum sacra deprehendas ac superstitionum persuasiones; sermo haud multum diversus, in deposcendis periculis eadem audacia et, ubi advenere, in detrectandis eadem formido. Plus tamen ferociae Britanni praeferunt, ut quos nondum longa pax emollierit.

11. As is usually the case among barbarians, no one's quite sure whether it was natives or foreigners who first colonised Britain.

Because Britons vary so much in looks, you can draw some conclusions. The Caledonians' red hair and large limbs point to a German origin. As for the Silures in the west, their dark skins and usually curly hair – and the fact that Spain is opposite them – suggest that Iberians crossed the Channel a long time ago and occupied the area. The Britons nearest to the Gauls look like them; either because they share blood, or because the climate in places so close to each other has produced similar physical characteristics.

I think that the Gauls probably did invade this nearby island. Their religious practices can be traced to the British taste for superstition; their language is much the same; both countries like facing up to danger and tackling it head on. Britons are more aggressive, though, as you'd expect in people who haven't been softened by years of peace.

12. *Caelum crebris imbribus ac nebulis foedum; asperitas frigorum abest.*

Dierum spatia ultra nostri orbis mensuram; nox clara et extrema Britanniae parte brevis, ut finem atque initium lucis exiguo discrimine internoscas. Quod si nubes non officiant, aspici per noctem solis fulgorem, nec occidere et exsurgere, sed transire adfirmant.

12. The British sky is obscured by constant rain and cloud, but it never gets really cold.

The days are longer than ours; the nights are clear and in the extreme north so brief that there's barely a dark moment between dusk and dawn. They say that, as long as the clouds don't get in the way, you can see the gleaming sun throughout the night; it doesn't set or rise, but just crosses the sky

The Roman occupation of Britain went well for a few years until, in 61 AD, the Britains revolted. Tacitus explains why in chapters 15 and 16:

15. *Namque absentia legati remoto metu Britanni agitare inter se mala servitutis, conferre iniurias et*

interpretando accendere: nihil profici patientia nisi ut graviora tamquam ex facili tolerantibus imperentur.

15. After the Roman ruler left and they were no longer scared, the Britons began to get worked up about their servitude, to compare their sufferings and exaggerate them.

"We only get treated worse by being long-suffering," they said. "Much more is asked of people who give way easily."

16. His atque talibus in vicem instincti, Boudicca generis regii femina duce (neque enim sexum in imperiis discernunt) sumpsere universi bellum; ac sparsos per castella milites consectati, expugnatis praesidiis ipsam coloniam invasere ut sedem servitutis, nec ullum in barbaris [ingeniis] saevitiae genus omisit ira et victoria.

16. The Britons got each other going with this sort of fighting talk and they declared war on us. They were led by Boadicea, a woman of royal blood – the Britons are indifferent to sex when it comes to royal succession.

They attacked our troops who were thinly scattered across our garrisons. They stormed our forts and they invaded our colony, which they thought of as the heart of their servitude. Burning with triumphant anger, the barbarians gave full rein to their savagery.

After the Romans suppressed Boadicea's rebellion, things calmed down in Britain. Tacitus wrote, in the following chapters, how the Romans went about recolonising the country, not by force, but by culture – by getting the native British upper-class to ape Romans by taking baths, eating banquets and wearing the toga.

21. *Sequens hiems saluberrimis consiliis absumpta. Namque ut homines dispersi ac rudes eoque in bella faciles quieti et otio per voluptates adsuescerent, hortari privatim, adiuvare publice, ut templa fora domos exstruerent, laudando promptos, castigando segnis: ita honoris aemulatio pro necessitate erat.*

Iam vero principum filios liberalibus artibus erudire, et ingenia Britannorum studiis Gallorum anteferre, ut qui modo linguam Romanam abnuebant, eloquentiam concupiscerent.

Inde etiam habitus nostri honor et frequens toga; paulatimque discessum ad delenimenta vitiorum, porticus et balinea et conviviorum elegantiam. Idque apud imperitos humanitas vocabatur, cum pars servitutis esset.

21. The following winter we introduced measures to calm things down. Agricola set up temples, markets and housing developments to ensure that these uppity barbarians scattered across the country got used to a quiet life of leisure and pleasure. He rewarded anyone who was hard-working and laid into anyone who was lazy. So people started to compete against each other to behave well; they didn't have to be forced to be good any more.

Agricola also set up a liberal education system for the sons of the gentry. He showed such a preference for the inventive British over the dogged Gauls that the British – who used to hate speaking Latin – fell in love with the language.

They even fell for our fashions and started wearing togas. Little by little they were drawn to things with a touch of sinfulness to them: drawing rooms, hot baths, elegant dinner parties. In their stupidity they called all this civilisation when it was all part of their servitude.

THIS AND THAT

The nice-sounding *hic, haec, hoc* – "this" and *ille, illa, illud* – "that" are horribly irregular but pretty crucial. Say *hic, haec, hoc* very quickly and it develops a sort of pleasant poem of its own. Not true of *ille, illa, illud.*

	Masc.	Fem.	Neut.
NOM	hic	haec	hoc
ACC	hunc	hanc	hoc
GEN	huius	huius	huius
DAT	huic	huic	huic
ABL	hoc	hac	hoc

PLURAL

	Masc.	Fem.	Neut.
NOM	hi	hae	haec
ACC	hos	has	haec
GEN	horum	harum	horum
DAT	his	his	his
ABL	his	his	his

	Masc	Fem	Neut.
NOM	*ille*	*illa*	*illud*
ACC	*illum*	*illam*	*illud*
GEN	*illius*	*illius*	*illius*
DAT	*illi*	*illi*	*illi*
Abl	*illo*	*illa*	*illo*

PLURAL

	Masc.	**Fem.**	**Neut.**
NOM	*illi*	*illae*	*illa*
ACC	*illos*	*illas*	*illa*
GEN	*illorum*	*illarum*	*illorum*
DAT	*illis*	*illis*	*illis*
ABL	*illis*	*illis*	*illis*

While we're on the subject of fiddly little words that are pretty crucial, here is another one – *is, ea, id* – he, she, it or that thing:

	Masc.	Fem.	Neut.
NOM	*is*	*ea*	*id*
ACC	*eum*	*eam*	*id*
GEN	*eius*	*eius*	*eius*
DAT	*ei*	*ei*	*ei*
ABL	*eo*	*ea*	*eo*

PLURAL

	Masc.	Fem.	Neut.
NOM	*ii/ei*	*eae*	*ea*
ACC	*eos*	*eas*	*ea*
GEN	*eorum*	*earum*	*eorum*
DAT	*eis*	*eis*	*eis*
ABL	*eis*	*eis*	*eis*

THE SUBJUNCTIVE, I'M AFRAID

If anything is designed to make the blood freeze, the subjunctive is a quite brilliant fridge.

The subjunctive is the only thing in Latin which really is properly difficult and doesn't respond to the clinical logic that dictates most of its otherwise lovely neatness.

No one's quite sure what the subjunctive means in English, and, to make it even more complicated, it has all sorts of odd little uses in Latin. Best to think of the subjunctive first of all as the "Let it Be" word. Just on its own, with no warning, it usually has an obligatory force, i.e. "let the record state", "let him go" would use a subjunctive.

A notable example is *Vivat regina…*, "Long live the queen," or, literally, "Let the queen live." Or *Caveat emptor* – "Let the buyer beware."

Then it's best to think of the subjunctive as the woulda/shoulda/coulda form; i.e. when there's a "would" or a "should" or a "could" around, it's a pretty good bet that you should use a subjunctive. Not always, but as a rule of thumb. (I fear I would lose you forever if I were to write out all the myriad bits of the subjunctive. Let me stick here to its definition and usage – for conjugation tables, Kennedy's your man.)

IF CLAUSES

So the subjunctive applies when you use "if" – that is, in a conditional clause, but only if there's an element of uncertainty signalled by woulda/shoulda/coulda.

"I'd love it if you would come to a little drinks I'm having for Jeffrey Archer."

That takes the subjunctive – because you're unlikely to take up the invitation. If, however, there's no woulda/shoulda/coulda, and there's certainty in the conditional clause, you don't use the subjunctive. The sentences – "If I go to the little drinks you're having for Jeffrey Archer, I will top myself out of a mixture of hatred and irritation." – takes a normal verb because you will certainly top yourself, or you are at least giving a strong impression that you will do so.

"ORDERING SOMEONE ABOUT" SUBJUNCTIVES

As you'll know from above (*supra*), when you tell someone to do something directly – "Get off my land," "Go and see the headmaster and take the strangled stick insect with you" – that's an imperative.

But if you're then telling the story about how you told somebody off – "I told Prince Charles to get off my land", "Mr Chips told Biggins minor to go and see the headmaster and take his strangled stick insect with him" – then you use the subjunctive.

The "to" in "I told Prince Charles to..." is translated by "*ut*".

Now, don't be put off by *ut*. It's a horrible-sounding word and is used to mean several different things, which is a bit daunting at first. But just translate it as "to" to begin with and you won't go too far wrong. Then, as you go through its different uses, you'll get better at handling it.

This use of the subjunctive is also called an indirect order.

CRUCIAL LITTLE WORDS

You must know your prepositions and conjunctions, the little words that glue clauses and phrases together. Some consolation: they crop up so often that you'll soon pick them up in passing without having to learn them.

There are two groups of prepositions, those that take the accusative, and those that take the ablative.

Prepositions that take the accusative:
Ad – to, at

Adversus – against

Ante – **before** (easily remembered by gamblers – the ante is the bet that all poker players must lay BEFORE a hand is dealt)

Circum – **around** (thus circumference, circumnavigate, etc)

Circa – **about** (abbreviated to c. in English: "I weigh c.10 stone, give or take 5 stone")

Extra – **outside, without** (this has confusingly mutated into meaning more of something; its original meaning is better seen in words like extradite, meaning "to place outside")

Infra – **below** (used in footnotes in English books)

Inter – **between** (thus intercourse, interfere, interpolate)

Intra – **within** (a precise, useful distinction from inter; thus "*Eum inter cordem iecurque confodi*" – "I stabbed him between the heart and the liver" – and "*Eum intra cordem confodi*" – "I stabbed him in the heart.")

Iuxta – **next to** (thus juxtapose)

Ob – **because of** (easily remembered by switching ob around, to get b.o., because of)

Per – **through** (thus perambulate, peradventure)

Post – **after** (thus post mortem, posterior)

Prope – **near**

Propter – **because of**

Supra – **above** (again used in footnotes in English books)

Trans – **across** (thus the Trans-Siberian Express, transfer, transvestite – literally across-clothes, from *trans* and *vestis, is f.* – *clothes*)

Ultra – **beyond** (mutated now in English to mean bloody huge, but still recognisable in its old form in words like ultramontane authority – the power exercised by popes beyond the mountains, i.e. on the southern side of the Alps)

VOCAB.

cor, cordis n. – heart

iecur, iecoris, n. – liver (considered the supposed seat of the passions by the Romans, especially love and anger)

confodio, -ere, confodi, confossum – I stab

Prepositions that take the ablative:

A, ab – by, with, from

Cum – with

De – about, concerning

Ex, e – from (thus extract, exude)

Prae – in front of

Pro – before, in front of (thus proclaim, proffer)

Sine – without

Sub – under (thus subterfuge, submarine)

Super – over (mutated to mean "above all else"; thus Superman)

There are also some confusing prepositions that take the ablative when applied to something at rest and the accusative when applied to movement towards:

In – in, on (ablative); into, onto (accusative)

Conjunctions

These again are crucial and again crop up so often that they gradually lodge in your mind. No need to learn them, then.

Et – and

-que – and (when tacked on to the end of a pair of nouns, *-que* joins them to mean "and": thus "Morecambe Wiseque")

Neque – nor

Etiam, quoque – also

Aut – either, or

Sed – but

Enim, nam – for

Ergo, igitur – therefore (*igitur* tends to be used at the beginning of a sentence; *ergo*, like in English, halfway through – "I fancied her, ergo I tried to give the impression I couldn't care less about her." Thus *Cogito ergo sum*, Descartes' axiom, "I think therefore I am")

Tamen, autem – however

Tandem – at last (easily remembered: "'Tandem', cried the old man who had been waiting for ever for a bicycle that carried two people")

Ut – so that

Quod – because

Cum – since

Dum – while
Donec – until
Si – if
Postquam – after that
Modo, tantum – only
Ubi – when

BEWARE THE MARCH OF IDS –
ROMAN DATES, NUMBERS, WEIGHTS AND MEASURES

The Roman way of doing dates was incredibly complicated and therefore provides a good example of the axiom – which I've just invented – that if something survived from Roman days, like pillars or words or central heating, then the Romans did it well; if something hasn't survived, like the Roman year, then they did it badly.

So we needn't really bother with Roman dates except for a few show-off points.

The Romans had several festival days in each month. The Kalends (incidentally one of the very few Latin words that begins with a "k") was on the first of the month. On the Kalends, interest was paid, and so it came to be called *tristes Kalendae*, "sad Kalends", that is, sad for debtors, marvellous for creditors.

The *Nones* tended to be on the fifth day of the month.

And the big one, the only one you need to remember, is the Ides, around about the middle of the month. For most purposes all you'll need to know is the Ides of March, which falls on the 15th.

"Beware the Ides of March," said a soothsayer to Julius Caesar, getting the date of his assassination at the hands of Brutus and Cassius in 44 BC spot-on. 2045 years later, a *Daily Telegraph* sub-editor was equally percipient about another doomed politician when he came up with the headline, "Beware the march of IDS."

THE JOY OF SEX, AND OTHER ROMAN NUMERALS

Roman numerals are a rare exception to my axiom, *supra* – only the good things survive from ancient Rome. They are unwieldy and not nearly as neat as Arabic numerals but they are useful for dates, monuments and showing off. They are also very easy to learn.

Numbers 1-10 go:

I II III IV V VI VII VIII IX X

The important ones there are V – 5 and X – 10. If you want to do one less than these, you put a I in front; one more, and you put a I after. And this principle goes on all the way up through the other new letters:

So XX is 20. XIX is 19. XXI is 21.
C (for centum) is 100. XCIX is 99. CI is 101.
D is 500. L is 50. DL is 550. DLI is 551.
M is 1000. And, if you want to go an adding 1000s, you go on adding Ms. So the year 2000 is represented by MM. The year 2006 is MMVI. And so on.

While we're on the subject, the numbers when written as words are very tricky in Latin because, like most words that are regularly used, they've become battered and irregular. One, two and three are the only numbers that decline:

Unus – one – is nice and straightforward, going *unus, una, unum,* like *dominus, mensa* and *bellum.*
Duo – two – is pretty odd, going *duo, duae, duo.*
Tres – three – is completely unpredictable, going *tres, tres, tria.*

As with Roman numerals, once you have learnt the written numbers of one to ten, you are pretty much there. From then on, they use combinations and permutations of those numbers. So:

1 – *unus*

2 – *duo*

3 – *tres*

4 – *quattuor*

5 – *quinque*

6 – *sex*

7 – *septem*

8 – *octo*

9 – *novem*

10 – *decem*

11 – *undecim* (i.e. combination of *unus* plus *decem*)

12 – *duodecim* (*duo* plus *decem*)

13 – *tredecim*

14 – *quattuordecim*

15 – *quindecim*

16 – *sedecim*

17 – *septendecim*

18 – *duodeviginti* (i.e. two short of twenty)

19 – *undeviginti* (one short of twenty)

20 – *viginti*

21 – *unus et viginti*

22 – *duo et viginti*

28 – *duodetriginta* (i.e two short of thirty)

30 – *triginta*

40 – *quadraginta*

50 – *quinquaginta*

60 – *sexaginta*

70 – *septuaginta*

80 – *octaginta*

90 – *nonaginta*

100 – *centum*

200 – *ducenti*

1000 – *mille*

With these few rules, a whole new world of tombstones and dates opens up. Epitaphs are always in very simple Latin, and the blast of smugness you get from being able to translate them, combined with the warm glow of remote mourning, is pretty powerful, particularly if there's someone with you who's impressed by that sort of thing.

The best example is in St Peter's, Rome, in the joint tombstone to the last three members of the Stuart family, kept from the throne by their Catholicism, their place taken by William and Mary.

James II's son, the Old Pretender, James Stuart, his son, Bonny Prince Charlie, and his nephew, Henry Stuart, who became a Cardinal, are all buried in the crypt of St Peter's, some way from the monument. The memorial is often littered with flowers, left by Jacobite romantics.

On the monolithic, white marble obelisk, with bas relief

portraits of the three men designed by the Roman sculptor, Antonio Canova, the inscription treats James Stuart as if he had been king:

JACOBO III JACOBI II MAGNAE BRIT. REGIS FILIO KAROLO EDUARDO ET HENRICO DECANO PATRUM CARDINALIUM JACOBI III FILIIS REGIAE STIRPIS STUARDIA POSTREMIS ANNO.MDCCCXIX

To James III, son of King James II of Great Britain, to Charles Edward and to Henry, Dean of the Cardinal Fathers, sons of James III, the last of the Royal House of Stuart. 1819.

Below the inscription are two weeping angels, symbolising the lost hopes of the exiled Stuarts.

Opposite the monument to the Royal Stuarts is a monument to Maria Klementyna Sobieska, wife of James Francis Edward Stuart and mother of Charles Edward Stuart and Henry Benedict Stuart. Its inscription reads:

MARIA CLEMENTINA M. BRITANN. FRANC. ET HIBERN. REGINA

Maria Clementina, Queen of Great Britain, France and Ireland.

The reference to France is a relic of the Plantagenet claim to the French throne.

Incidentally, a decade ago, when the Canova marble was beginning to look a little tarnished, an appeal went out among Jacobite supporters to clean it up. The chief contributor ended up being that secret Jacobite Queen, the Queen Mother, who couldn't hide the Scottish roots planted in her birthplace, Glamis Castle in Forfar.

TO YOU, GUV, THAT'LL BE 23 SESTERTII – ROMAN MONEY, WEIGHTS AND MEASURES

Money

The most famous Roman coin was the *sestertius*, which literally means "two and a half" because there were two and a half asses – the copper *as* was the basic unit of Roman currency – to a sestertius, a silver coin.

The *quinarius*, also silver, was worth five asses or two *sestertii*; the *denarius*, ten asses, or four *sestertii*.

Weights and Measures

Our British Imperial measures are still pretty much based on Roman measures with a few tiny differences over the intervening two millennia.

After the Romans left Britain, the Anglo-Saxons introduced their own measures – furlongs, yards, acres, pecks and bushels. And then, after the Norman conquest, the Normans reintroduced Roman measures, resulting in a system that mixed ancient Anglo-Saxon measures and Roman measures.

These units were standardised by Magna Carta in 1215 and were periodically reviewed and updated (notably in 1496, 1588 and 1758). It was the UK Weights and Measures Act of 1824 which finalised our measurements as they stand today.

As for those Roman measures, they were as follows:

The Roman *libra*, also called, confusingly, the *as* or a *pondo* – thus our pound – was equal to about 12 ounces.

The *amphora*, as in an ancient two-handled clay jug, was also a measure of liquid – a Roman cubic foot, equivalent to about seven gallons.

The Roman *pes* or foot, equivalent to about 11.6 inches, derived from the rough length of an adult male foot, is roughly the length of our modern foot measurement.

The longer unit, a *stade*, is equivalent to 625 Roman feet, or 607 imperial feet.

INDIRECT STATEMENTS

One of the most useful things about learning Latin is that it introduces you to the detailed study of grammar and syntax – something that is almost completely absent these days from the teaching of English.

So far, we've mostly looked at the different endings that Latin words have according to their role in the sentence. Now let's take a brief tour of just a few of the more common Latin constructions. We will start with indirect statements.

An indirect statement is when something that somebody said (or says, or might say, etc.) is being reported by the main sentence. So, suppose Aeneas says "Dido is miserable." We can report that statement in any number of ways:

Aeneas tells me that Dido is miserable.
I don't believe that Dido is miserable.
Surely it's no surprise that Dido is miserable.

Different languages have different ways of performing this important trick, although you'll also find that most languages have several different ways of doing it. English likes to use "that", and to repeat the original statement almost verbatim. In fact, we often even leave out the "that", which seems to make our method especially simple: Aeneas says Dido is miserable.

In Latin, the preferred construction looks like this:

Aeneas says Dido to be miserable.

Dido, in this case, becomes a quasi (*quasi* – sort of) object of the verb "to say" (and so goes into the accusative case) and the verb goes into the infinitive (retaining the tense of the original statement).

Aeneas dicit Didonem miseram esse.

I say Cicero has an incredible nose.
Dico Ciceronem nasum incredibilem habere.

He said Carthage had to be destroyed.
Dixit Carthaginem delendam esse.

I think it's time for a drink.
Credo nunc esse bibendum.

Caesar said he had come, seen, conquered.
Caesar dixit se venisse, vidisse, vicisse.

Princess Diana kept saying that MI6 were trying to kill her.

Diana, mulier regii generis, dictitabat homines sicarios et reginae servos se occidere velle.

In the last examples, the reporters of the statement (Caesar and Diana) themselves appear in the reported statement. So it comes out like this: "Caesar said *himself* to have come, to have seen, to have conquered." "Diana kept saying assassins to be trying to kill *herself*." So you find a *reflexive* pronoun ("herself", "himself"): se.

Incidentally, this way of doing things might seem rather exotic, but it really isn't. It's fairly common in English as well: I believe him to be innocent. I know it to be true. He considered himself to be one of us. I take all this to be obvious.

I WANT ALWAYS GETS SOMETHING TRICKY

Simple desires just take the infinitive. So, "I want to kiss Cameron Diaz," is just, *Cameronam Diazam osculari volo.*

But, if you want Cameron Diaz to do something more complicated, involving a whole new clause, then you have to use: "*ut* plus the subjunctive". This is called an indirect wish.

"I want Cameron Diaz to deny that I'm a stalker."

Volo ut Camerona Diaz neget venationes amatorias meas sibi molestas fuisse.

Here you come across one of the nice pleasures of Latin – that it allows you to come up with new words for objects invented since Roman days, and to have a proper think about what the real meaning is behind a particular word.

The Romans didn't have stalkers – if you look at the Rape of the Sabine women, they didn't need to be half-hearted about these things. Shortly after the founding of Rome in 753 BC, the Romans found that there were many more men than women in the city, so they promptly invaded the next door city, where the Sabines lived, and took all their women.

The Rape of the Sabine Women, Nicolas Poussin, c.1635

Given that the Romans had no need, and so no word, for something as furtive (*fur, furtis, m.* – a thief) as a stalker, we have to invent a word for it.

The expression I've used above for stalking is "*venatio amatoria*" – "a love hunt". So the sentence literally means, "I want Cameron Diaz to deny that my love-huntings bothered her."

SCARED OF THE SUBJUNCTIVE

Fear clauses also use "*ne* plus the subjunctive":

"I'm bloody terrified that my ex-wife will go back to her childhood sweetheart."

"Timeo ne uxor ad amatorem pueritiae redeat."

VOCAB.
uxor, uxoris m/f. – husband/wife
pueritia, -ae, f. – childhood
redeo, redire, redii, reditum – I return
timeo, -ere – I fear
amator, -is – lover

When you're reporting that somebody asked somebody else a question, the verb in the question they ask goes in the subjunctive:

> James Whitaker, the *Mirror*'s royal reporter, alias the Fat Tomato, asked Andrew Morton when Camilla travelled to Highgrove in the boot of Charles's Aston Martin.

> *Jacobus Whitaker, Speculi regalis nuntius, alias obesus Tomato, Andream Mortonum rogavit quando Camilla, in Caroli Astonis Martini tergo celata, in Altasilvam iter fecerit.*

VOCAB.

rogo, -are – I ask

speculum, -i, n. – mirror

regalis, -e – royal

nuntius, -i, m. – messenger

alias of course translates into alias. From *alius, -a, -um* – another, other, different, *alias* literally means "at another time"

Altasilva – Highgrove, literally "High wood"

tergum, -i, n. – back

iter facio – I make a journey.

celatus, -a. -um – hidden

While we're on the subject of questions, here are the main question words you'll need:

Quis – **who, what.** This is the interrogative pronoun, and it will be useful to know how it declines:

SINGULAR

	Masc	Fem	Neut.
NOM	quis/qui	quis/quae	quid/quod
ACC	quem	quam	quid/quod
GEN	cuius	cuius	cuius
DAT	cui	cui	cui
ABL	quo	qua	quo

PLURAL

	Masc.	Fem.	Neut.
NOM	qui	quae	quae
ACC	quos	quas	quae
GEN	quorum	quarum	quorum
DAT	quibus	quibus	quibus
ABL	quibus	quibus	quibus

Incidentally, it is from this pronoun that the ancient game of "Quis? Ego" derives. I say ancient because it has all but completely died out, except among Wankers. It was a simple game. A prep school boy would hold a *Figurine Panini* sticker of Kevin Keegan up in the air and shout to the whole classroom, "Quis?" The first boy to answer "Ego" ("Me"), got the sticker.

Quando – **when.** Familiar from the Englebert Humperdinck song of the same name: "Tell me when will you be mine, tell me, quando, quando, quando."
Ubi – **where**
Quam – **how**
Quantus – **how big**
Quotiens – **how often**
Qualis – **of what kind**
Qualis – **of what type**
Uter – **which of two**

All these direct question words take an indicative verb, i.e. the simplest kind, as we see below when Juvenal lists the questions put to him by a drunken thug on the street one evening:

"Unde venis?" exclamat, "Cuius aceto,
Cuius conche tumes? Quis tecum sectile porrum
Sutor et elixi vervecis labra comedit?"

"Where have you come from?" he shouted, "Whose off wine and beans have you been stuffing yourself with? Which cobbler has been eating sliced leeks and boiled sheep's lips with you?"

Juvenal, Satires III, On Life in Rome

VOCAB.

acetum, -i n. – vinegar

conchis, -is f. – bean

tumeo, -ere – I swell, am swollen

sectilis, -e – cut, sliced-up

porrus, -i m. – leek

sutor, -oris m. – cobbler

elixus, -a, -um – boiled

vervex, -ecis m. – sheep

labrum, -i n. – lip

comedo, -esse, -edi, -essum – I eat up

Things change slightly when you use "which" or "what" in the middle of a sentence, as opposed to in a question – i.e. "He loved the bus which went through Chelsea". Here you use the relative pronoun, *qui, quae, quod,* meaning "the one which" or "the one who": "*Currum amavit qui per Chelseam iit.*"

Currus, -us m. strictly means chariot. Our word "bus" comes from a Latin-derived word, "omnibus", which wasn't actually used by the Romans. It comes from the dative plural of *omnis, -is, -e* – meaning "all, every".

The name was coined by a wit, very possibly a Wanker, who, when asked what the big thing full of people was for, said, "It's 'for everyone' – i.e it's an 'omnibus'."

Anyway here is how you decline *qui, quae, quod*. It only varies from *quis, quis, quid* above in the nominative and accusative cases:

NOM	*qui*	*quae*	*quod*
ACC	*quem*	*quam*	*quod*

NUM AND NONNE QUESTIONS

You use "*num*" to introduce direct questions to which you expect the answer, "no"; and "*nonne*" for questions to which you expect the answer, "yes".

Matthew Norman put it well in the *Daily Telegraph* on 3rd October, 2005,

> Have you ever seen a match in which captaincy played a decisive part? (If you have, no letters please: that was what Latin teachers used to know as 'a question requiring the answer "No"'.)

As opposed to:

If Fergie's interviewed in *Hello!*, will she say something stupid?

Si Ferga in Ave! interrogabitur, nonne aliquid stultum dicet?

VOCAB.
ave – hello, hail
miror, -ari – I wonder
stultus, -a, -um adj. – stupid

YOU HORRIBLE LITTLE MAN

Latin has a lovely way with diminutives, i.e. turning a normal thing into a smaller thing: as a rough rule of thumb you add *-ulus* on the end:

"We've got this marvellous little man who comes in daily to massage my wife's head."

"*Hunc homunculum mirabilem habemus, qui quotidie venit ut uxoris caput terat.*"

I'LL LOVE YOU SO MUCH THAT I'LL LEARN CONSECUTIVE CLAUSES FOR YOU

The above heading is a consecutive clause. Whenever you think something or someone is so lovely/horrible/odd smelling that something happens as a consequence, use the subjunctive for the consequence, with the "that" translated by "*ut*".

The failed writer hated Jemima so much that he drank all her wine at the party for her book, *Liberate your Cellar Space.*

Scriptor incognitus Jemimam adeo oderat ut, cum in illo convivio adesset, in quo novum suum libellum ea recitabat, qui nomen habet 'Libera Cellam Tuam', omne eius vinum ipse biberit.

Or, more properly:

Iam res Romana adeo erat valida ut cuilibet finitimarum civitatum bello par esset.

Now Rome was so strong that, when it came to war, it was on a par with any of the neighbouring states.

Livy, *History of Rome I.IX,*
The Rape of the Sabine Women

validus, -a, -um – strong

quilibet, quaelibet, quodlibet – anyone, anything

finitimus, -a, -um – neighbouring

par, paris – equal

YOU LEARN FINAL CLAUSES IN ORDER TO BECOME ATTRACTIVE TO THE OPPOSITE SEX

Whenever you do something "in order to" do something else, Latin expresses that purpose by putting the verb into the subjunctive, and the "in order to" is translated by *ut*.

Again, "in order to" has a touch of Wanker's English, and is more usually encountered just as "to":

"Honestly, officer, I only drank the bottle of Calvados to calm my nerves after the crash."

"*Sincere, praefecte, Calvadi amphoram modo bibi ut metus meas post magnum meum periculum sublevarem.*"

VOCAB.

quotidie – daily

caput, capitis n. – head

tero, terere, trivi, tritum – I rub

destitutus, -a, -um – destitute

odi, odisse – I hate

convivium, -i, n. – party, feast (thus "convivial")

bibo, bibere, bibi, bibitum – I drink (thus "imbibe")

sincere, the adverb from *sincerus, -a, -um* – honest

praefectus, -i, m. – officer, prefect

YO, ROMANS – LATIN INTERJECTIONS

There are plenty of Latin words to suggest shock. But there are only two you really need to know:

Eheu – "alas" (as in Horace's 'Fogey's Lament' from his *Odes* – *Eheu, fugaces anni labuntur* – Alas, how the years slip by, see WHEN IN ROME, *infra*)

Ecce – "look", "lo and behold" (familiar to many Latin prep-school veterans in the depressingly jocular and second-rate exercise book, *Ecce Romani!*, its mock laddish quality best translated as "Yo, Romans!")

GOLDEN LATIN –
OR HOW TO WRITE LIKE CICERO

Even though it's much better to dissolve compact, staccato Latin into chatty, free-flowing English, there are some lovely little Latin writing devices which, in both Latin and English, nicely loosen up the language. (You can tell, from their Greek names, that a lot of these flourishes were dreamt up by the Greeks and nicked by the Romans.)

Under Cicero in the first century BC, Latin hit top form, as the great Roman lawyer developed the figures of speech that still work today in written English, as well as in speeches.

There's a handy element of showing-off in knowing all the names of these little devices – assonance, hendiadys or whatever – but the key thing is to be able to use them. They are properly effective in English.

Alliteration – Use of consonants that have similar sounds.

Anacoluthon – Cutting short the first of two expressions to give the impression of haste or boredom: "I said that I would love her for ever, that diamonds and roses…, but she went home with Brian."

Aposiopesis –When the obvious conclusion of a statement is left out.

"The thing is, Deirdre, I think about you a lot, and I've never said this to a girl before, but…"

Res est, Deirdre, de te cogito multum, et puellae hoc nunquam antea narravi, sed…

VOCAB.
de (plus ablative) – about
nunquam – never
narro, -are – to say

Apostrophe – Confusingly, as well as meaning ', apostrophe also means a statement, often a question, addressed to someone or something not present:

Ubi est, mors, stimulus tuus?
"Death, where is thy sting?" (1 Corinthians 15:55)

Assonance – Repeated use of vowels, to give a pleasing sound effect.

Asyndeton – The omission of conjunctions to produce a powerful combination of compression and flow, eg *Veni, vidi, vici*. This was a device much used by Churchill, however unenthusiastic he was about Latin at Harrow (cf. THE CASES – OR CHURCHILL'S PROBLEMS WITH A TABLE, *supra*).

In his "We shall fight them on the beaches" speech on June 4th, 1940 in the House of Commons, Churchill listed ten separate "We shall…" clauses until he used his first 'and' as a conjunction between those clauses:

> We shall go on to the end, we shall fight in France, we shall fight on the seas and oceans, we shall fight with growing confidence and growing strength in the air, we shall defend our island, whatever the cost may be, we shall fight on the beaches, we shall fight on the landing grounds, we shall fight in the fields and in the streets, we shall fight in the hills; we shall never surrender.

Asyndeton can get a bit tiring. Evelyn Waugh certainly thought so. It was exactly this sort of portentous pile of little Latinate clauses that made Waugh have the character Guy Crouchback, the protagonist of *Men At Arms*, call

Churchill "a master of sham Augustan prose".

By Augustan prose, Waugh meant the so-called Golden Age of literature, which extended from 80 BC to 14 AD, reaching a peak under the Emperor Augustus, with Virgil, Horace, Ovid and Livy. Intricate and varied as those writers were in their poetry and prose, the neatness and precision of their Latin meant that a "sham" version of it reduced it, in Waugh's eyes, to a series of simple, leaden platitudes.

Ellipsis – Ellipsis just means missing words out, leaving them to be understood by the reader. The most common form of ellipsis is with the verb "to be", often left out for reasons of style and compactness. Say "*Paris Hilton bella*", and a Roman will know you're saying Paris Hilton "is" beautiful. Ellipsis is also used of certain adjectives where the noun is so expected that it's understood, like *dextra, sinistra* (right, left), which understand the word *manus* – hand.

Incidentally, many dialects of English also leave out the verb "to be": in black American, "she fine" or "You crazy"; in newspaper headlines, "Richard Burton dead"; in signage, "Exit at rear".

If you want to say whose mother or father somebody is, you don't need to include the words "son of" or "daughter of". So you would say, *Charles Elizabethae* (*filius* understood) or *Beatrice Fergianae* (*filia* understood).

Hendiadys – Using a noun as an adjective. So "*vi et armis*" literally means "with power and weapons", but the force of it is really "with powerful weapons".

This is a trick that isn't much good in English: if you want to use an adjective, use one; ditto with nouns.

Hysteron-proteron – Putting the thing that happened second first for dramatic tension. The expression is from the Greek for "later-earlier", and gave its name to the Hysteron-proteron club at Oxford, the one that liked to begin its meals with cigars and Calvados and finish with soup, breadsticks and aperitifs. e.g:

Moriamur et in media arma ruamus.
Let us die and rush into the thick of things.

Virgil, *Aeneid* II. 353

Litotes – understatement. This often means using a negative to take the edge off a positive, as often employed by Anthony Powell, i.e."not uninteresting" to mean "really quite interesting". e.g:

Quaerite non sani pectoris auxilia.
Seek help for a mad [literally, "not sane"] heart.

Propertius, *Elegies, Cynthia*

Metaphor and Simile – Exactly the same as in English but, once you think in classical terms, it's easier to remember that a metaphor (from the Greek, "to transfer") suggests that some day-to-day object actually *is* some extraordinary out-of-this-world other thing; while a simile (from *similis, -e* – similar) is *like* some other thing. So:

> *Caesar ab Italia volantem*
> *remis adurgens, accipiter velut*
> *mollis columbas aut leporem citus*
> *venator in campis nivalis*
> *Haemoniae.*

Caesar rushed after Cleopatra as she flew over the sea from Italy, like [i.e a simile] a hawk after soft doves or a hunter sprinting after a dove on the plains of snowy Thessaly.

Horace, Odes I: XXXVII, The Fall of Cleopatra

If Horace had missed out the *velut* – "like", this would have been a metaphor.

VOCAB.
volo, -are – I fly (as in Dean Martin's *Volare*)
remus, -i m. – oar

adurgeo, -ere – I pursue closely

accipiter, -tris m. – a hawk

mollis, -e – soft (as in "Mollify")

columba, -ae f. – dove (thus columbarium, a tomb with niches holding urns of ashes, like a dovecote)

lepus, -oris m. – hare

citus, -a, -um – swift

venator, -oris m. – hunter

campus, -i m. – plain

nivalis, -e – snowy

Haemonia, -ae f. – the old name for Thessaly

Metonymia – The replacement by a dull word of one with more of a flourish, often with the name of its related god, i.e. referring to dance as Terpsichore, or war as Mars.

WARNING: This is a device often used by the camp and unfunny, by second-rate poets, and the pompous and over-weight, and must be used sparingly. The dangers are best caught in the Regency series of *Blackadder* where Blackadder runs into Shelley and Byron at Mrs Miggins's Coffee House, in ruffed shirts, loudly calling for "the juicings of the naughty bean."

A rather more classy example:

Quis post vina gravem militiam aut pauperiem crepat?

Quis non te potius, Bacche pater, teque, decens Venus?

After wine, who bangs on about grave war or poverty?
Who wouldn't prefer to talk about you, father Bacchus,
or you, charming Venus?

Horace, Odes 1.37, The Blessings and Dangers of Wine

VOCAB.
crepo, -are, crepui, crepitum – chatter
potius – rather

Oxymoron – Putting together two apparent opposites (from the Greek for "sharp-stupid"), e.g:

Nobby Stiles homo parvus magnus Mundi Calicis erat.
Nobby Stiles was the little big man of the World Cup.

Paronomasia – Using similar-sounding words with different meanings.

Tibi parata sunt verba, huic verbera. (Tacitus)
For you words have been prepared; for this man, blows.

Periphrasis – The use of a long phrase when a short one would do – is not unlike metonymia, and is equally dangerous.

Nox caelum tundit, mox nobis castra ponenda.

Night bruises, and we shall be forced to camp. (Uncle Monty in *Withnail and I* when it begins to get dark on the fells.)

Pleonasm – The use of pointless words, as in:

Humphreius Bogartus Laurenam Bacallam labellis osculatus est.
Bogart kissed Bacall on the lips.

Polyptoton – Different cases of the same noun are dragged together.

Iam clipeus clipeis, umbone repellitur umbo;
ense minax ensis, pede pes et cuspide cuspis. (Statius)

And now shield was repelled by shield, shield-boss by shield-boss, threatening sword by sword, foot by foot and spear-point by spear-point.

Incidentally, *cuspis, is m.* – spear-point – is where we get "cusp" from. Being on the cusp of something is often uncomfortable.

Prosopopeia – The personification of abstract qualities, also highly dangerous, and favoured by pseuds. E.g

O, Iuventus, Iuventus, Iuventus dulcis; ubi es?
Oh, Youth, Youth, Sweet Youth; where are you?

VOCAB.
Iuventus, -utis, f. – the prime of youth, as well as the name of Italy's Turin-based football team (once you turn the I to a J, as the Italians often do – the Romans didn't use Js).

The name, Juventus, was coined by an appropriately young group of fourteen to seventeen-year-olds from the D'Azeglio High School in Turin, who formed a team on November 1, 1897, using the black and white-striped shirts of Nottingham County Football Club to play in.

The Romans were nice and charitable about youth, and considered the prime of youth to last from the age of twenty to 45.

Synecdoche – Using the part of an object to describe the whole. We do it in English – calling a car "a motor". The Romans did it a lot: *caput* (head) for *homo* (man); *carina* (keel) for *navis* (boat).

While we're on the subject, we get our word "nave" from *navis* – from the ship-shaped (or, more confusingly, keel-shaped) wooden roof over the central spine of the church.

Tricolon – Listing things in threes, a real favourite of Cicero's. It's a trick taken up by comedians ("There's an Englishman, an Irishman and a Scotsman...") and Hollywood scriptwriters (every episode of *Friends* and practically all other decent sitcoms have three separate plotlines).

Zeugma – Using a single verb or adjective in two different ways, e.g.

Rem et eam manu accepit .
He took her point and took her by the hand.

WHEN IN ROME, TALK AS THE ROMANS TALK –
A LATIN PHRASEBOOK

A few years ago, the English law courts decided to do away with Latin because it was confusing some of their clients. Lawyers were up in arms, saying that there was no concise way of translating Latin expressions like *mutatis mutandis* ("after making the necessary changes"). Well, lawyers may have found Latin clearer than English. I doubt that their clients agreed.

All the same, there are a lot of Latin expressions which still survive and, while they're dying out, their use can still give you that I-know-this-and-you-don't glow.

Adeste fideles – "O come, all ye faithful!"
The hymn was originally in Latin, origin unknown.

Ad hoc – "For this purpose"
A genuinely useful word, meaning temporarily useful, i.e.

212

"Michael Howard was an ad hoc leader of the Tory party". "Wrapping up the shower-head with sellotape is a perfectly good ad hoc way of stopping it leaking, darling, till I can be bothered to go down to Jewson's for a new one."

Ad hominem/ad rem – "Dealing with an individual/dealing with an issue"

An *ad hominem* attack on Margaret Thatcher's reign as Prime Minister would take her as a whole and tend to be abusive, viz. the man who beheaded her statue in the Guildhall in 2002.

An *ad rem* attack would take the form of a learned *Guardian* op-ed by Polly Toynbee on the pitfalls of the poll tax and union-busting legislation.

Ad infinitum – Indefinitely

Literally, "until infinite", memorably coined by Jonathan Swift.

So, the naturalists observe, the flea,
 Hath smaller fleas that on him prey;
And these have smaller still to bite 'em;
And so proceed, ad infinitum.

Ad libitum – Off the cuff

Better known as *ad lib*, it literally means "at pleasure", but is most commonly used of the improvisation technique of the stand-up comedian, so there may not be much pleasure involved in the process.

Ad nauseam – Endlessly
Literally, "until sickness", used of things that go on and on: "As we entered the year 2020, the torrent of reality TV programmes continued ad nauseam."

Advocatus diaboli – "Devil's advocate"
Also known as the *promotor fidei*, the "promoter of the faith", the devil's advocate is employed by the Vatican to argue against a beatification or canonisation.
Also used of the wilfully contrary, viz. John Humphrys, Jeremy Paxman.

Aegrotat – The malingerer's degree
Literally "He is sick." This is the name for an unclassified degree given to a student who is too "ill" to do his exams.

Alea iacta est – "The die is cast"
Said by Caesar when, during his 49 BC battle with Pompey, he crossed the Rubicon, the river separating Cisalpine Gaul from Rome – the point at which he knew there was no

going back, that war was inevitable.

Alias – Originally meant "at another time". Mutated to mean "also known as".

Alma mater – "Nourishing mother"

Used to mean your old university. The Romans used it to describe Ceres, goddess of agriculture, and Cybele, the nature goddess.

Alumnus – "Nursling, foster child"

The graduate of a particular university.

Amicus curiae – "A friend of the court"

Once used in law to mean a professional who isn't party to the litigation but is brought into court to give advice.

Anno Domini – "In the year of our Lord"

Abbreviated to AD.

When you write, say, 1987 AD, the literal translation is "In the Lord's 1987th year". This explains why there was never a year zero between 1 BC and 1 AD. In this Christian dating system, modelled on years of emperors' reigns, you could hardly say, "In the Lord's noughth year" or "The noughth year of the reign of Nero."

Annuit coeptis – "He has favoured our undertakings"

May only ring bells with Americans. Taken from the *Aeneid*, this line is on the back of the great seal of the United States, and the back of the $1 bill.

As is often the case, Latin is used to give a touch of class (always John Rockefeller IV, not John Rockefeller 4, which sounds like half a football score).

Ante meridiem – "Before noon"; thus a.m. and p.m. or ***post meridiem***

Apologia pro vita sua – "A defence of his own life"

Apologia is in fact a Greek word, meaning defence, which has mutated into the word apology – although, for those who realise that the quickest way to get out of responsibility for something is to apologise without meaning it, it still is a sort of defence.

Apologia pro vita sua was the title of Cardinal Newman's autobiography (1864)

A posteriori – "From what comes after"

An *a posteriori* truth is something, derived from experience or investigation, that turned out to be true, or that we discover to be true by investigating the world: e.g. that human beings evolved from apes.

To be contrasted with an *a priori* argument – "from what comes before". An *a priori* truth is one that is immediately obvious, without the need for any investigation of the outside world: e.g., that 2 + 2 =4, or that I cannot both be, and not be, in Rome.

A priori: Alcohol ruins the liver; Paul Gascoigne drinks heavily; therefore he must have a bad liver.
A posteriori: Paul Gascoigne has a bad liver; bad livers are usually caused by alcohol; therefore Gascoigne probably drinks heavily.

Arma virumque cano – "I sing of arms and the man"
The first line of the *Aeneid*. *Arms and the Man* is also the title of a George Bernard Shaw comedy (1984). It is also the only line that most classicists can remember, and therefore the only line that bluffers need remember.

Ars gratia artis – "Art for the sake of art"
The credo ("I believe", incidentally) of the high-minded artist, and the MGM studio, seen above the roaring lion at the opening of all their films.

Ars longa, vita brevis – "Art is long, but life is short"
This is the Latin version of a saying thought up by

Hippocrates (as in the Hippocratic Oath). Hippocrates meant that the amount that a doctor needs to figure out is vast, and life is short — i.e. too short to figure it all out. This was a recognition of the limitations of our knowledge and abilities, typical of the intellectual humility of the Greek enlightenment. What he was saying was, "Life is short, mastering the art is long."

The saying has now changed its force to mean that artistic creations live on long after the death of their creators.

The expression is a good example of the Latin phobia of the verb "to be". Quite often it's missed out altogether, to make things sound neat and trim.

Aura popularis – Fleeting fame

This literally means the "popular breeze", used by Cicero of anybody who's the people's favourite for a while.

Aura has mutated into meaning a sort of mystical charm that lasts slightly longer than the average wind blows for.

Ave atque vale – "Hail and farewell"

Said by Catullus on his brother's death:

Atque in perpetuum, frater, ave atque vale.
"Hello and goodbye forever, brother."

Could also be used by the sufficiently confident/pompous on bumping into somebody in the street you don't want to talk to very much.

Ave Maria – "Hail Mary"

The angel's annunciation to the Virgin, telling her of impending motherhood, from Saint Luke's Gospel. The full text is:

> *Ave Maria, gratia plena, Dominus tecum. Benedicta tu in mulieribus, et benedictus fructus ventris tui, Iesus. Sancta Maria, Mater Dei, ora pro nobis peccatoribus, nunc, et in hora mortis nostrae. Amen.*

> Hail Mary, full of grace. The Lord is with thee. Blessed art thou amongst women, and blessed is the fruit of thy womb, Jesus. Holy Mary, Mother of God, pray for us sinners, now and at the hour of our death. Amen.

Benedictus benedicat – "May the blessed one give a blessing"

The shortest form of grace before eating.

Say under breath, just loud enough to be heard by your neighbour at dinner if you want to give off an accidental impression of holiness and a public school education.

Bona fide – "In good faith"

Used of transactions which often end up going wrong but were meant with the best of intentions. *Bona fide* is in the ablative.

The nominative works too – when Eddie Murphy picked up a transsexual prostitute, it was a *bona fides* transaction on his part, since he believed he was paying the going rate for a pretty woman. It was a *mala fides* (bad faith) transaction on hers/his. Well, that's if you believe that Eddie Murphy's press statement was bona fide.

Carpe diem – "Seize the day"

From Horace's *Odes*,

Dum loquimur, fugerit invida Aetas:
carpe diem, quam minimum credula postero.

As long as we're talking, hostile time is fleeing: so get a bloody move on, instead of hanging around hoping for something better to turn up.

And from PG Wodehouse's *Much Obliged, Jeeves:*

"Carpe diem, the Roman poet Horace advised. The English poet Herrick observed the same sentiment when he suggested that we should gather rosebuds while we may. Your elbow is in the butter, sir."

Casus belli – The justification for making war

Much used at the opening of the war in Iraq in 2003, but in use for centuries before.

Thomas Aquinas wrote extensively about the circumstances in which war, particularly a holy war, was justified.

Caveat – Warning

Literally, "let him beware", *caveat* is used as a warning when you should be aware of the exception to the rule. E.g.,

"The Adelaide beaches are long, sandy and sun-kissed. There is a caveat – Great Whites like them too."

Caveat emptor – "Let the buyer beware"

The shopkeeper's cry and, for a long time, the traditional position in law: it was up to the purchaser to make sure he was getting what he wanted before buying it. After that, he had no redress.

More and more, with the rise of the guarantee and the growth of consumer protection law, it's more like *Caveat venditor* – "Let the seller beware."

Cave canem – "Beware of the dog"

Sign outside Roman suburban villas. The original mosaic is in Pompeii, the well-heeled Surbiton of Italy (*supra*).

Cf – Look

Originally an abbreviation for *confer*, which in Latin meant "compare".

Used to mean, "look elsewhere in this list I've given you". So, in a dictionary of Rock and Roll, you might have the entry:

Sayer, Leo – cf. "Stars, Washed-up 70s." [*pace* his Number One Hit (UK) in 2006, the remix of Thunder in My Heart].

Codex – A manuscript

Originally spelt caudex, it meant "tree trunk". Came to be used to mean a book of wooden tablets, with words inscribed into a block of inlaid wax (not, as Asterix would have it, carved out of stone blocks).

Other useful book terms are:

Folio – edition, as in Shakespeare's first folio. From *folium* – *leaf*, which mutated into *folium* – page.
Verso – the left-hand page in a book (from *folio verso* – "the page having been turned", meaning the first page

you look at after turning).

Recto – the right-hand page, from *rectus, -a, -um* – not, annoyingly, meaning right-hand, but from *rego, regere, rexi, rectum,* meaning to guide or direct. So *recto folio* means "with the page set straight".

Coitus interruptus – Self-explanatory

From *coitus, -us m.* – a meeting. Can also mean "a coming together", but not always. Depends on participants.

Cornucopia – "The horn of plenty"

This crops up in a lot of Renaissance paintings, where some lucky virgin or similarly blessed figure carries round a horn the size of an old gramophone speaker, stuffed with flowers, fruits of the forest and cornsheaves.

The idea comes from Amalthea, the goat that suckled the young Zeus. In return, the grateful Zeus gave the goat the power to produce whatever it wanted out of its horn.

Corpus iuris – "Body of law"

The collected laws of a country.

The expression used to have more weight abroad, particularly in France and its old colonies, like Louisiana, which depended on a body of codified law, called in fact Roman Law.

Britain and a body of law didn't originally go together. We used to depend for our law on the slow build-up of case law or common law combined with the accumulation of government bills in statute law.

But the gradual incorporation of European Union statutes and conventions into our law means that more and more we could be said to have a *corpus iuris*.

Cum laude – "With praise"

Much more widely recognised in America, where the expression *magna cum laude* – "with great praise", is used of the second best degrees. *Summa cum laude*, "with greatest praise", is used of the best, while the not very good students are informally awarded degrees *summa cum difficultate* – "with the greatest difficulty".

Curriculum vitae – A CV

This literally means "the course of your life", which shows what careerists the Romans are; that the sum total of your existence is reduced to what you got in your O-Levels, whether you were a team player during your holiday job in the local Waitrose and how quick your typing speed is.

De facto – In reality

A way of distinguishing from *de iure* – "according to the

strict letter of the law". So: "The *de iure* Prince of Wales is Prince Charles. The *de facto* Prince of Wales is Tom Jones."

De gustibus non est disputandum – "There is no disputing about tastes"

A rare use of the gerund, literally meaning, "It is not to be disputed about tastes".

If you want to show off and imply that this is the sort of expression you use the whole time, even if nobody else does, it's enough to say, "De gustibus…", and leave the rest of the expression hanging in the air:

"There's no question about it. Blue and the Darkness rule. De gustibus…"

Dei gratia – "By the grace of God"

Delenda est Carthago – "Carthage must be destroyed"

Said by Cato during the Third Punic War (149-146 BC), after several centuries of Carthage being public enemy number one. Good sort of expression to be used by those who want to seem powerful in a world-weary way and are finally exerting the power they've always had.

"Look – we've been to your mother-in-law for Christmas for 37 years in a row. I've just got to go to Arsenal-Spurs on

Boxing Day this year. *Delenda est Carthago.*"

Delirium tremens – "Trembling delirium"
Used of the hallucinations and shakes of heavy drinkers.
Often abbreviated to the DTs.

De mortuis nihil nisi bonum – "Speak nothing but good
about the dead"
One of the great lies: see behaviour of Romanian peasantry
on the death of Nicolae Ceaucescu; uncontained joy in
London on suicide of Adolf Hitler, 1945.

Deo volente – "God willing"
Often abbreviated to D.V. "Dale Winton's contract for pre-
senting Pick of the Pops on Radio Two on Sunday afternoons
won't be renewed, D.V."

De profundis – "From the depths"
Usually of despair. Taken from Psalm 130 – "Out of the
depths have I cried unto thee, O Lord."
Also the title of the letter written in prison by Oscar Wilde
to the man who'd got him there in the first place: his lover,
Lord Alfred Douglas.

Deus ex machina – "A god out of the machine"

The fallback of the desperate writer, who suddenly wants to tie up the end of a story with the extraordinarily unlikely appearance of somebody who explains the whole plot:

> "Clearly, Lewis, it must have been Professor Wormbridge that did it. He's just published a paper in the *New Scientist*, explaining how he's the only man on earth who knows how to make a new form of strychnine out of Oxford's house ink."
>
> "That's a bit of a *deus ex machina*, isn't it, Morse?"

From the practice of lazy ancient Greek dramatists who liked to land a God on stage with a mechanical crane at the end of their plays to explain everything.

Domine, dirige nos – "Lord, guide us"
The motto of the City of London.

Dramatis personae – "The persons of the drama"
The cast of a play.

Ecce homo – "There's the man"
The words spoken by Pontius Pilate (John 19.5) as he pointed to Jesus in his crown of thorns.

e.g., exempli gratia – "For the sake of example"

Should be used only to introduce an example, not, like *i.e.*
i*d est*, "that is", to expand on and explain what you're talking
about.

Eheu fugaces labuntur anni – "Oh, how the years slip by"

From Horace's *Odes*. Can be neatly shortened to *Eheu
fugaces*, whenever you see something that makes you feel old:
policemen getting younger; your friends appearing in obituar-
ies; your first intimations that nightclubs are not really that
enjoyable.

Emeritus – "Honorary", "well-earned"

An emeritus professor won't do a full professor's job but is
given the title as a reward for long service.

Ergo – "Therefore"

As in: "The junior head of accounts in Lillysmith's paints
was deeply disgusting to secretaries and odiously sycophantic
to his bosses; *ergo* he got promoted."

Seems a bit pompous because you might as well say "therefore" instead of ergo. But it has a nice axiomatic quality to it,
implying that this is always the way with junior heads of
accounts, secretaries and bosses.

Erratum – "Mistake"

The errata slip in a book will list as many mistakes as the publisher has found after the proof has gone to the printers.

Et al. – "And the other people"

Short for *et alii*.

Etc – Abbreviation for *et cetera,* meaning "and the other things" (NB two words; pseuds might want to pronounce them as such.)

Et in Arcadia ego – "And I too have lived in Arcadia"

Arcadia, in the Greek Peloponnese, was a blissful rural idyll. This inscription is found on a tombstone in a Poussin picture. It's also a chapter heading in *Brideshead Revisited,* the one where Charles Ryder has a good time at Oxford.

Et tu, Brute – "You too? Brutus?"

Brutus is in the vocative here and should also be in deep disgrace for turning on his old friend, Caesar.

Can be used of any once loyal friend. "Et tu, Geoffrey Howe?" (Margaret Thatcher, October 1990).

Awkwardly, from the point of view of this book singing the praises of Latin, Caesar actually spoke to Brutus in Greek, and said something slightly different: "*Kai su, teknon?"* – "You too, my child?"

Ex cathedra – "With authority". Literally "from the chair".

When a pope speaks *ex cathedra*, he is speaking in his official capacity, and ergo infallibly. Can be used in other contexts:

> "Young Michael Owen should be shot for that foul."
> John Motson was not speaking *ex cathedra* when he made that remark on *Match of the Day* last night.

Exeat – Holiday

Literally "let him be absent", *exeat* was first used for priests allowed out of the monastery for a few days. Later used for schools and universities.

Exeunt/Exit – The characters or character walk/s off stage.

A useful stage direction.

Ex libris – From the library of…

Literally "From the books of". Usually found in bookplates.

Ex officio – "By virtue of office"

An entitlement to some job or another by virtue of your

grand standing in some other job. So:

"Because she was the Queen, she was *ex officio* chief of the clan McTavish with special proprietary duties for the upkeep of the Western Stromness lighthouse."

Ex post facto – "After the fact"

E.g., "The Sky studio was full of *ex post facto* experts on 1st September 1997, saying it was mad to drive through Parisian underpasses at 160mph with a drunk chauffeur at the wheel."

Ex tempore – Off the cuff

Literally "of the time", often used as an adjective: an *ex tempore* speech.

Festina lente – "Hurry slowly"

i.e. If you want to get things done quickly, do them slowly.

Used by Suetonius of Augustus, who very slowly turned Rome from a republic to an empire, with none of the rebellions that might have happened if he'd done it quickly.

Fidus Achates – Loyal friend

Used by Aeneas of his best friend, "faithful Achates", who was always doing his best to cheer up his boss when the task of founding Rome was looking like an uphill task.

Floruit – Golden period

Literally, "he flourished" from *floreo, -ere, -ui* – "bloom", "flower".

Used particularly of artists and writers, and often as an abbreviation (Evelyn Waugh, fl. 1925-60; Pam Ayres, fl. 1975-9).

Fons et origo – The original source

Literally, "the fountain and origin". Used particularly of pioneers: "Hugh Hefner was the *fons et origo* of the porn industry"

Habeas corpus – A protection against arbitrary imprisonment

Literally, "you must have the body" (from the present subjunctive of *habeo: habeam, habeas, habeat…*). The "*habeas corpus*" writ is a cornerstone of British and American law. It means that any person must be brought before a court – i.e. "you must have the body" in court – and have his case investigated before he's put in jail.

Ibid. – "In the same place", short for *ibidem*

Very useful when compiling lists or anything where a long expression is repeated, particularly, say, in the explanation of the location of footnotes at the end of a scholarly book:

"Chapter 7

1. *Sexing Shakespearean Hermeneutics and the Other,* page 27.

2. ibid., page 31."

Can be used in other contexts: "On May 1st, I found Peter O'Toole in the Plasterers' Arms, sitting next to a table covered with empty glasses of Chablis spritzers. On May 2nd, I bumped into Peter O'Toole (ibid.). Three years later, I ran into Peter O'Toole (ibid.)."

In flagrante delicto – Caught red-handed
Literally "in the middle of a burning crime". Used of crooks and surprised lovers.

Infra dignitatem – "Beneath your dignity"
Shortened to *infra dig.* to mean naff or rude, below the belt.
"All I did was say your Peugeot 405 had failed its MOT. Punching my teeth out was a bit *infra dig.*"

In loco parentis – "In the place of a parent"
E.g., "We've been using ITV in loco parentis for 20 years and Nigel seems perfectly well-adjusted."

In medias res – Straight to the meat of it

Literally, "in the middle of things", used of arriving suddenly in the thick of it:

"David Cameron was elected leader of the Conservative party on December 6, 2005, and soon found himself *in medias res* when Jeffrey Archer begged to be let back into the party."

In memoriam – "In memory of"

In nomine Patris et Filii et Spiritus Sancti – "In the name of the father, the son and the Holy Ghost"

Inter alia – "Among other things"

E.g.: "The pub bore in the Albion touched on, *inter alia*, how MI6 had killed Princess Diana and the fact that the druids had moved the bluestones of the Preseli Mountains by astral humming to Stonehenge."

In vino veritas – You tell the truth when you're drunk

Literally "In wine, the truth."

In vitro – Artificial

Literally, "in glass", and so used of test-tube babies. As opposed to "in vivo" – taking place in a living organism.

Ipso facto – Because of that very thing

Literally "by the fact itself".

"You work for the bank. The bank works for me. Ipso facto, I'm your boss."

Ben Stiller, Dodgeball [2004]

The expression tends to be used of self-contradictory statements, where the fact of the statement being made itself contradicts the content:

If you have to explain how funny your joke was, then, ipso facto, it wasn't funny.

If you have to ask yourself if you love me, then, ipso facto, you don't.

Lex primae noctis – *Droit de seigneur*

Literally "the law of the first night", the entitlement of a lord to go to bed with a serf's wife on her wedding night. It says much for English prudery that there is no English expression for this.

Lex Salica – "Salic Law"

The law of the Salian Franks, who lived in the north of modern Germany where the Rhine meets the North Sea. Salic

Law is usually known for its refusal to let women inherit estates.

Litterae humaniores – Classics, the first two years of classics at Oxford

Literally, "more humane letters", *lit. hum.* as it is abbreviated to, covers the greatest hits of classics – poetry, prose, history and philosophy.

The exam of the same name at Oxford was the longest exam in the world – thirteen three-hour papers in a week – before it was superseded by the Chinese Civil Service Exams (or so people like me who've sat them like to claim).

The Chinese Civil Service Exams have in fact been around for several thousand years. To begin with, they tested music, archery, horsemanship, arithmetic, writing and knowledge of the rituals of public and private life. They later expanded to include military strategies, civil law, revenue and taxation, agriculture and geography in addition to the Confucian Classics. By 1370 each sitting of the exams could be as long as 72 hours on the trot.

Locum tenens – A substitute

Literally "holding a place", the expression is shortened to *locum*, for people with a temporary position, usually doctors or vicars. Note that the words shifted in French to *lieu-tenant*.

Magister Artium – "Master of Arts"

Abbreviated to MA – the degree one above a BA.

Magnificat – A song of praise

Literally, "it magnifies", from the Virgin Mary's response to the Annunciation:

Magnificat anima mea Dominum
"My soul magnifies the Lord."

Magnum opus – A masterpiece

Literally, "a big work".

Mea culpa – My fault

Literally, "by my fault", being in the ablative. To add emphasis, say "*mea maxima culpa*" – my fault in spades.

Medicinae Doctor – "Doctor of Medicine"

Abbreviated to MD.

Memento mori – Remember that you must die

Literally "remember to die", used of an object that reminds you of your mortality – a skull, your fading grandfather, a ticking clock.

Mens sana in corpore sano – Healthy body, healthy mind

Literally, "healthy mind in healthy body", an idiom coined by Juvenal in his *Satires*, i.e. exercise is good for you.

Modus operandi – A way of working things out

Literally, "a way of working" – *operandi* is a gerund here (from *operor, -ari* – to work) – used normally of a compromise, a third way.

Modus vivendi – "A way of living"

Again, normally used of a compromise and, again, *vivendi* is a gerund here (from *vivo, vivere* – to live). So, "I was keen on watching *Wife Swap*. She preferred listening to Bach. So we established a *modus vivendi*, where we agreed never to be in the drawing room at the same time."

Ne plus ultra – The best

Literally, the "no more further", it tends to be used of things that are far and away the best in their field, no contest.

"Terry Wogan is the *ne plus ultra* of the broadcasting constellation."

Nil desperandum – Don't worry

Literally, "nothing is to be despaired about."

The "is" is understood in the expression. *Desperandum* is a gerundive. The expression was used in Horace's *Odes*.

Non omnis moriar – "I shall not altogether die"
Used in Horace's *Odes* to declare that his works would live on after him.

Non sequitur – An illogicality
Literally, "it doesn't follow".

"His name," said Flick, "is Roderick Pyke. That's why I'm running away."

This struck Bill as a *non sequitur*. Women do eccentric things, but surely the most temperamental girl would hardly leave her home simply because a man's name was Roderick Pyke."

P.G. Wodehouse, *Bill the Conqueror* [1924]

Novus ordo seclorum – "A new order of the ages"
This motto is printed on the back of the dollar bill, with the implication that a new order was born on the invention of the United States. While we're on the subject, America's motto is *e pluribus unum* – one out of many, i.e America was formed out of lots of separate states.

Nunc dimittis – "Now you may leave"

Taken from *Nunc dimittis servum tuum, Domine* – "Now send your servant away, Lord" (St Luke).

Used of any official permission to leave.

Obiit – "He died"

Abbreviated to ob. in people's dates (George Best, fl. 1966-68, ob. 2005). See "floruit" – *supra*.

Obiit sine prole – "Died without issue"

Abbreviated to o.s.p. in genealogy reference books.

Oderint dum metuant – "Let them hate, as long as they fear"

The motto of the boss from hell, and the Emperor Tiberius.

Odi et amo – "I hate and love"

Catullus sums up intense passion.

Pace – Respectfully disagreeing with

Literally means "at peace", though that doesn't help very much, e.g. "*Pace* Prince Charles, organic food can be disgusting and modern buildings can be OK."

Pari passu – "At the same pace"

Used to describe two enterprises being treated in the same

way. For e.g., "We've been using the construction of Wembley Stadium as a template for our builders. *Pari passu*, we should have plumbed in the sink by 2025."

Passim – "Everywhere"
Used in particular of literary works.
"The tendency for novelists to start using familiar words for new meanings, like "sock" for flat and "rug rethink" for haircut (Martin Amis, *passim*), is a relatively new phenomenon."

Paterfamilias – Patriarch
Literally, "the father of the family".

Pax Romana/Britannica – "Roman/British peace"
Used to describe peace imposed on a grand scale. Often used now of Pax Syriaca – Peace in Syria.

Pecunia non olet – "Money doesn't smell"
The rallying cry of financiers worldwide. Ernest Saunders, Anthony Parnes, Robert Maxwell *et cetera*.

Per ardua ad astra – "Through perils to the stars"
The motto of the RAF.

Per capita – "Individually"

Literally, "by the head".

Per impossibile – Hypothetically

Another useful expression confined to Latin that doesn't quite transfer to English. It means, "assume the impossible".

"Imagine, *per impossibile*, that you were faithful to your wife, Lord Archer, and that you were offered a million pounds to sleep with another woman."

Per se – In and of itself

Literally, "through itself", the expression is used to denote some hidden aspect of an object.

This is how the restaurant, Per Se, overlooking Central Park in New York, one of only four restaurants in the city with three Michelin stars, got its name. Its chef, Thomas Keller, available to cater private parties at $300,000 a throw, was asked if his new, as yet unnamed restaurant, would be similar to his California restaurant, the French Laundry: "It won't be the same, per se," Keller said. And the name stuck.

Persona non grata – "An unacceptable person"

Because we're more interested in stories about gatecrashers than life-enhancers, *persona non grata* is used much more often than the expression it grew out of, *persona grata*.

Post mortem – "After death"
An autopsy.

Post partum – "After birth"
From *partus, -us, m.* – a birth.

Post scriptum – "After having been written"
As in PS, from the past participle of *scribo, scribere, scripsi, scriptum* – I write.

Prima facie – "At first appearance"

Primus inter pares – "First among equals"
Used when somebody is chosen as the leader of a group of equally qualified people. The leader may have extra powers allotted to him in order to carry out his duties, but he is in no way considered superior to his contemporaries.

Pro bono publico – "For the public good"
The fuller version of *pro bono*, as in *pro bono* lawyers who do work for free.

Pro forma – For form's sake
Literally, "for form", "pro forma" is now most regularly used of an invoice sent to a buyer in advance of the ordered goods.

Pro rata – "In proportion"

Qua – "In the capacity of"

Derived from the ablative feminine singular of *qui* – who or what.

"Dr Murgatroyd was most encouraging. He said the spots qua spots… Is it qua?"

"Perfectly correct, sir."

Bertie Wooster and Jeeves in P.G. Wodehouse's
Aunts aren't Gentlemen (1974)

QED, quod est demonstrandum – "The thing that is to be proved"

This expression was originally used in maths problems. You would be given some equation, say, $e=mc^2$, and then once you'd proved it, you'd write QED at the end. Then the expression came to be used in arguments:

"Ben Elton is a genius."

"No, he's not."

"Look at *Blackadder*."

"Read his novels or some of his recent stand-up, after the double-seat sketch. QED."

Quid pro quo – Something for something

Literally "What for what?"

E.g., "If I come to the James Blunt concert with you, there's got to be a *quid pro quo* – am I allowed not to come shopping with you tomorrow?"

Quis custodiet ipsos custodes? – "Who will guard the guards themselves?"

Juvenal, in his *Satires*, was referring to the problem of finding men to guard women suspected of infidelity while their husbands were out of town.

Now the expression is more often used of people in powerful positions who then abuse that power.

"What can you do when the Trade and Industry Secretary lies on a mortgage form and does special favours for foreign billionaires? *Quis custodiet ipsos custodes et Petrum Mandelsoniam?*"

Quondam – "Former"

Used as an adjective, but only by the pompous (cf. WANKER'S LATIN, Lord Patten of Barnes): "My *quondam* girlfriend did her nut when she saw me with her fat cousin."

Quos deus vult perdere prius dementat – "Those whom a god wishes to destroy, he first drives mad"

Derived from Euripides, this line was twisted by the English critic Cyril Connolly (1903-74) to "Those whom the gods wish to destroy, they first call promising."

He was referring not least to himself and the great burden of being thought brilliantly clever at Eton and being appointed a member of Pop, the school's society of the most popular boys; life was inevitably downhill from then on.

Cyril Connolly: those whom
the gods wish to like chips...

Quo vadis? – "Where are you going?"

Not just a bad 1951 film with Peter Ustinov as the Emperor Nero.

When St Peter was fleeing martyrdom in Rome, he met Christ on the Appian Way going in the opposite direction:

Dicit ei Simon Petrus, "Domine, quo vadis?"
"Quo ego vado non potes me modo sequi, sequeris autem postea."

Simon Peter said, "Where are you going, Lord?"
"I'm going where you can't follow me now, but you will later [i.e. to martyrdom]."

John, 13:36

Rara avis – A rarity
Literally "a rare bird", from Juvenal's *Satires* –

Rara avis in terris nigroque simillima cycno.
A rare bird in these lands and very similar to a black swan.

This was in the days when black swans were rare birds. The phrase has come to signify any sort of unlikely circumstance:

"A leader of the Tory party with a full head of hair? *Rara avis.*"

Re – Concerning
From *res, rei f.* – "thing", "matter", literally "in the matter of".

Reductio ab absurdum – "Reduction to absurdity"
The principle, mathematical or otherwise, of taking a statement to its logical conclusion, which turns out to be

impossible. E.g., "Plain-speaking is always good. Gerald Ratner."

Res ipsa loquitur – "The thing speaks for itself"

Often used as an axiom in English courtrooms before Latin was banished in the late 1990s. Quoted when a lawyer thought there was no need to prove something because it was so stark-staringly obvious.

At Jeffrey Archer's first libel trial in 1987 over his sexual acts with Monica Coghlan, the presiding judge, Bernie Caulfield, said of Mary Archer, "Has she elegance? Is she not fragrant?"

He was essentially saying "*res ipsa loquitur*", i.e. of course she was bloody elegant and fragrant and, that being the case, Jeffrey could have no conceivable need for, as Mr Justice Caulfield put it, "cold, unloving, rubber-insulated sex in a seedy hotel room".

As it turned out, *res ipsa non loquitur*.

RIP – Requiescat in pace – "May he rest in peace"

Nice use of the subjunctive.

Rus in urbe – "The country in town"

A corner of a city that brings memories of the country.

"Oh Marjorie, your suntrap behind the extension! Absolute *rus in urbe*!"

248

Can be used the other way round: *urbs in rure* – a little bit of the city in the country.

"Christ I got bored living in the Shetlands for a whole winter. I got Sky put in. Pure *urbs in rure* bliss!"

Seq. – Abbreviation for *sequens* and *sequentes*, meaning "the following", often used in notes for books, i.e. "cf. page 23 *et seq.*"

Sic – Meaning, when put in brackets in a quote, "Wrong, but that was how the original speaker said or wrote it."

For e.g., "No. That's how you spell 'potatos' [sic]." Dan Quayle, Munoz Rivera School, Trenton, New Jersey, 1992.

When the Duchess of York received a letter from a journalist, referring to her incorrect use of a word, quoting her with the word [sic] implanted, she angrily wrote back, "It's one thing to accuse me of getting something wrong; it's quite another to refer to my eating problems."

Sic transit gloria mundi – "Thus passes the glory of the world"

First written by Thomas à Kempis, in *De Imitatione Christi*, on the transitory nature of grand projects, it can be a useful show-off thing to say, ironically, at times of deep human shortcomings:

"Ginger Spice made a dame? *Sic transit…*"

Silent leges enim inter arma – "Laws go quiet in wartime"
An axiom from Cicero's *Pro Milone,* often quoted by critics of George Bush when they write about Guantanamo Bay or the state bugging American citizens.

Si monumentum requiris, circumspice – "If you seek a monument, look around you"
The inscription on the tomb of Sir Christopher Wren in the crypt of St Paul's, his masterpiece.
Often used in a heavy-handed way by journalists: "Thierry Henry. *Si monumentum requiris, Highbury circumspice.*"

Sine die – Until an unspecified day
Literally "without a day", a way of saying things aren't going to be resolved for some time. E.g., "After he had won the school maths and computing prize, Nigel resolved to get a girl-friend *sine die.*"

Sine qua non – A crucial condition
Literally "without which not".
"The *sine qua non* of going to stay with your mother-in-law in Hunstanton on Friday is that we leave by Saturday lunch and no later. And we're not having lunch."

Stet – "Let it stand"

A sub-editor's mark by a crossed-out word or sentence that he wants reinstated. From the 3rd person singular subjunctive of *sto, stare, steti, statum* – I stand.

Sub iudice – Still before the courts

Literally "under judgment", the words are a legal term, meaning that you can't say something prejudicial about somebody before their trial is concluded.

Sub poena – "Under punishment"

Much used in American cop shows – "We'll slap a *sub poena* so fast on him, he'll think he's drowned in Latin" –– the expression derives from English law, meaning a writ summoning someone to appear before court with a specified punishment if they do not appear.

Sui generis – A one-off

Literally "of its own kind", this tends to be used not as a term of flattery, but as a precise way of denoting an oddity that doesn't fit the norm.

E.g., "When it comes to parking restrictions in Britain, London is *sui generis.*"

Tabula rasa – A blank slate

Literally, "a writing tablet that has been scraped", used of an empty mind or of a place without history.

Te deum – "A devotional hymn"

An abbreviated version of *Te deum laudamus* – "We praise you, Lord". Also called the Ambrosian Hymn, because of its association with St Ambrose (340-397 AD), a popular Bishop of Milan who was keen on the *Te Deum*.

Tempus fugit – "Time flies"

The Wanker's 25th birthday wail.

Terra firma – Dry land

Literally "firm land", popularly used by returning seafarers – "Great to be back on…".

Timeo Danaos et dona ferentes – There's no such thing as a free lunch

Literally, "I fear Greeks even when they're carrying presents," said by the Trojan priest, Laocoon, when he first saw the wooden horse that brought the downfall of Troy.

Ultima Thule – The end of the world

Literally "the end of Thule", from Virgil's *Georgics*. Thule was thought to be the northernmost island in the world, a six-day journey beyond Britain – the equivalent to Iceland.

Urbi et orbi – "To the city and the world"
The name for speeches made by the Pope to Rome and the world.

Vade mecum – "Go with me"
Something you carry with you every day. It originally referred to a favourite book, but would now be applied to a Blackberry or bottled water.

Velis nolis – "Whether you like it or not"
The origin of willy-nilly. As in this sentence, where Seneca is berating someone for not turning to Stoicism:

> *Tu occupatus es, vita festinat: mors interim aderit, cui velis nolis vacandum est.*

> You're busy, life is a rush: meanwhile death will be upon you, and you will have to make time for that, whether you like it or not.

Versus – "Against"
Abbreviated to v.
Confusingly, in legal circles, you write Jarndyce v. Jarndyce,

but in order to put one over on non-legal types, you *say*, "Jarndyce and Jarndyce". A rare example of lawyers choosing not to use Latin.

Via – "By way of"
The ablative of *via, -ae, f.* – way.

Vice versa – Conversely
Literally "the change being turned".

Video meliora proboque, deteriora sequor – "I see better things and approve of them, and end up doing the worse thing"
Originally from Ovid's *Metamorphoses,* the cry of the recalcitrant drunk and the aspiring novelist.

Viva voce – An oral test
Literally "with live voice", the idiom is often shortened just to *viva* and is usually a test conducted after an exam to classify a mark when it is on the borderline between, say, a First and a Second.

Martin Amis is one of the few Oxford undergraduates to receive a congratulatory viva for the outstanding First he got when he was at Exeter College. Summoned to the university's examination schools for a *viva*, he thought he was going to have to argue his right to a First over a Second. Instead, the gathered dons stayed quiet and just burst into applause.

Viz. – Namely

Short for *videre licet* – "One may see."

"The Tories have had one spectacularly successful bald leader, viz. Winston Churchill. But they've had many more bald failures, viz. William Hague, Iain Duncan Smith, Michael Howard."

Volenti non fit iniuria – "Injury can't be done to a willing person"

A legal concept that doesn't always hold true. In R v Brown [1993], a group of sado-masochists who had been happily nailing each other's testicles to the floor were convicted of actual bodily harm, after their defence of *volenti non fit iniuria* failed.

DUMBING UP, OR DEATH TO THE CAMBRIDGE
LATIN COURSE – A CONCLUSION

Whatever you think of Mel Gibson's drinking habits and supposed anti-Semitism, at least he tried with his Latin when it came to his film, *The Passion of The Christ* (2004).

There aren't many films with a credit for "Theological Consulting and Aramaic/Latin Translation", and Dr William J. Fulco, the Jesuit priest brought in to sort out the locatives and the subjunctives, gets an alpha beta, if not quite an alpha, for his homework.

The Latin is pretty straightforward, and certainly pretty understandable by anybody who's got this far in this book.

"*Sanctus est,*" is Mrs Pilate's view of Jesus. "*Facta non verba,*" is the Roman soldier's order to Christ, when he starts talking too much. "*Mortuus est,*" says Longinus, the soldier who sticks a spear in Jesus's side to check whether he's alive.

There's only one slip – noticed by the classicist (First in Classics, Balliol), Boris Johnson. If you are addressing a man from Judaea, you should use the vocative "Judaee", not "Judaeus", as was said in the film; *vide* Julian the Apostate converting to Jesus with his last, and grammatically correct, words, "Vicisti, Galilaee" – "You have won, O Galilean one."

Still, even Father Fulco's simple Latin will be beyond most schoolboys now. Latin in Britain is not quite yet a dead language. But it is dying. For all the supposed life that Harry Potter breathed back into the language, a negligible number of children are now learning it in any rigorous way.

Yes, they might be able to translate the Hogwarts motto – '*Draco dormiens numquam titillandus*' ('Never tickle a sleeping dragon').

But they won't be able to write a Latin poem in praise of Maggie Smith's acting skills or J.K. Rowling's philanthropy, or recite screeds of Virgil as any halfwit grammar school boy or public school boy could half a century ago.

The number of grammar schools has slumped in that time; and the number of children studying Latin in public schools and the remaining grammar schools has collapsed. In 1960, 60,000 children did Latin O level. Now 10,000 do the much more basic replacement, GCSE (and, of these, in 2004, only 3468 came from state schools.)

When it comes to A levels, it's time to drag in the life-support machine: only 5,000 children a year take a classical A level of any sort; that's less than 0.8 per cent of all A levels taken. And, if the future looks less than rosy for Latin, it's wine-dark for Greek. Fewer than a thousand children a year do GCSE Greek, squeezed out by its declining stablemate, Latin.

Of the three classical A levels (Latin, Greek and classical civilisation), it's easiest to score high marks for a correct translation in Latin. Yet the amount these few Latinists are expected to know about the mechanics of the language has withered away. Bye-bye to long summer afternoons spent in sweaty terror of chalk-stained bachelors slamming desk-lids down on your fingertips if you don't know the gerund of *caedo* (*caedendum*) or the Latin for a funeral feast (*silicernium*). Hello, *Cambridge Latin Course* – the evil Latin-for-idiots school textbooks, used in 80 per cent of schools which offer Latin.

The *CLC* says that learning things like cases, genders and vocabulary puts people off; much better, it thinks, to give you the translations at the bottom of the page and let you work out how the words fit together by feel.

The course just plain doesn't work: it's like dumping a carburettor, a spark plug and a windscreen-washer-fluid holder in front of you, and expecting you to build an engine out of them.

The *CLC*'s misguided, evil approach is along the lines of "Well, Latin's really too difficult to learn with all those odd declensions and conjugations, so let's serve it up to the kids in ready-sliced digestible bite-size pieces, and set it in a lovable family context, with everyday Pompeian countryfolk like Caecilius, Metella, their son Quintus, cook, Grumio, slave, and Cerberus the dog."

Will Griffiths, the director of the course, summed it up in 2005 by saying, "It's not as if pupils need to know about the passive periphrastic, is it?"

Well, of course they don't *need* to know about the passive periphrastic. For that matter, as far as the *CLC* is concerned, they don't need to know what the accusative is or the imperfect or the imperative are. The words are just plonked on the page with their immediate translation and no context, i.e. *Caecilius est in horto. Metella est in triclinio. Cerberus est in mensa. Eheu!*

If they wrote, for example, "*Willum* (or *Guilielmum*) *Griffiths stultum esse dixerunt*", the clues they give would be along the lines of *dixerunt* – they said; *stultum* – stupid; *esse* – was. There would be no hint as to why the perfect of *dico* is *dixi* or why its 3rd person plural is *dixerunt*. Or why *esse* actually means "to be", and why you have to use the infinitive here. And you would never learn along the way what an infinitive is, or the perfect tense, or an accusative.

Now, again, these are things that you don't *need* to know. In just the same way, you don't need to know the poems of

Thomas Hardy, or what evening light looks like on the cloisters of Salisbury Cathedral.

But, like the infinitive and the passive periphrastic, these are things that will improve you if you do have the good fortune to know them.

And, by the way, unnecessary as it might be to know what a passive periphrastic is, if you do know what it is, it shows a rare mastery of English.

If you're not interested in what it is, Will Griffiths, then you're not fit to be employed as director of a body that is supposed to be interested in the study of Latin.

Incidentally, in that last sentence, "you're not fit to be employed" is a passive periphrastic.

To form the passive periphrastic of "I employ"– *conloco, -are* (literally, "to place with") – you add the gerundive to the verb "to be":

"Tu, Guilielme, non es collocandus."
"Will Griffiths, you're not fit to be employed."

Will Griffiths's despicable argument is that there is simply no earthly need to learn Latin in the way that you have to learn maths, or English or how to wire a plug.

But there *is* a need to learn Latin – if nothing else, to enlarge your appreciation of beauty, along the lines put forward by Robin Williams's character in favour of poetry in the film *Dead Poets' Society*.

> We don't read and write poetry because it's cute. We read and write poetry because we are members of the human race. And the human race is filled with passion. Medicine, law, business, engineering, these are all noble pursuits, and necessary to sustain life. But poetry, beauty, romance, love, these are what we stay alive for. To quote from Whitman:
>
>> "O me, O life of the questions of these recurring, Of the endless trains of the faithless, of cities filled with the foolish... What good amid these, O me, O life?
>>
>> "Answer: that you are here. That life exists, and identity. That the powerful play goes on, and you may contribute a verse."

So, learn Latin first for its verses and its beauty.

But learn it also for its language-teaching skills; in that way it is a bit more like medicine, law, business, engineering and wiring a plug.

As Kingsley Amis has pointed out, it's wrong to think that learning Latin is a sort of "mental gymnastics", a specially designed exercise for strengthening the mind. It's also wrong to think that learning Latin will make your English better because the two languages share so much. In fact Latin is much more precise and neater than English – and so you, as the translator, have to make a conscious effort to jump from the register of one language to that of another. Unlike most modern European languages, Latin and English aren't easily swappable, word for word.

The other important quality of Latin is the very quality that it is usually blasted for – its deadness.

Because living languages are in a constant state of flux, there's a great deal of wriggle room when translating from one living language to another.

Precisely because Latin is dead, there's none of that flexibility: this doesn't mean you can't be free and easy with your translations, but it does mean that you are much more likely to be definitely wrong in your translation if you haven't understood exactly what a particular word means or how a grammatical rule works.

So, there's not really much point in doing Latin unless you do it properly and learn it from its first principles. Which is why the drastic lowering of standards for exams like GCSEs is so depressing.

When I did my O levels in 1986, we were asked to translate a fifteen-line chunk of a speech by Cicero to the Senate, *In*

Catilinam, attacking his enemy who conspired against Rome in 63 BC. And we'd never seen the passage before – that's why the exercise was called an "Unseen".

Ciceronian prose is nice pellucid stuff, full of lovely rhetorical tricks. In the passage we had to translate, Cicero demonstrated the ancient art of the tricolon: arranging words or phrases in triplets, often of ascending lengths, for dramatic effect:

> *Nunc te patria, quae communis est parens omnium nostrum, odit ac metuit et iam diu nihil te iudicat nisi de parricidio suo cogitare; huius tu neque auctoritatem vere-bere nec iudicium sequere nec vim pertimesces.*

Your native land, which is the mother of us all, hates you and dreads you and has long since decided that you have been planning nothing but her destruction. Will you not respect her authority, bow to her judgment, or fear her power?

Cicero, *In Catalinam*

And now what does the average sixteen-year-old have to do? Yes, he's given a chunk of Cicero, but he doesn't have to translate it word for word. All he does is answer a few spoon-fed questions on a book he's already prepared.

2004's GCSE passage concentrated on Cicero's speech about a conman called Pythius. Pythius had fooled a Roman gentleman, Canius, into buying a country estate with supposed excellent fishing rights by paying some fishermen to fish in front of the grounds on the day Canius inspected the property.

The questions were fantastically simple: "Who was Canius?"; "What kind of work did Pythius do?"

The only question that involved any translation was, "Pick out two Latin words which describe Canius and translate them."

Two words! Forget learning about tricolons, with three clauses building up to a crescendo. Even knowing three words is too much nowadays.

It's not all bad news. In America, which suffered a great slump in classics in the late twentieth century, there's a bit of a revival going on.

In 1905, 56 per cent of American high school students studied Latin. By 1977, a mere 6,000 pupils took the National Latin Exam. That went up to 134,873 in 2005.

But American Latinists have never been taught from the young age that British and European classicists used to be. In Donna Tartt's book about obsessive classicists, *The Secret History* (1992), the parvenu narrator, Richard Papen, gets some plus points when he turns up at the exclusive Hampden

College in Vermont, and reveals that he's done two years' Greek at the age of 18 – BUT HE'S DONE NO LATIN.

When I arrived at Oxford to do classics, I'd done eight years of Latin and seven years of Greek. That tradition of learning classics from the age of ten or eleven is dying, as teachers and curriculum devisers take the age-old, defective answer to people refusing to do something difficult; make it easier, to the point where you squeeze out all the value that comes from a difficult exercise precisely because it is difficult.

The Vice-Chancellor of Oxford and the proctors are still rigorous about the conduct of examinations: 'Rule (vi): Invigilators are strongly encouraged not to allow more than one person of each sex to go to the toilet at any time... Rule (xiv): Except for the drawing of diagrams, no candidate shall use pencil for the writing of an examination unless prior permission has been obtained from the proctors.'

But when it comes to how much Greek or Latin you need, the Vice-Chancellor and his proctors are pussy-cats.

When I did my Greek A level in 1988, we translated chunks of Herodotus out of 1950s O level papers to practise. Now, to get into Oxford to read the alternative Classics degree, Mods B, you don't need any Greek at all. Two years into the four year degree course, when all classics undergraduates used to have to be able to translate all 24 books of the *Iliad*, you can now get away with just books one, nine, 22 and 24.

If you want to get in to do a related classical subject, like Classical Archaeology and Ancient History, not only do you not need Greek; don't bother with Latin either.

It's going to get worse. Brilliant classicists don't become schoolmasters any more. All the men who taught me Latin and Greek at school, now in their forties and fifties, had been Oxbridge scholars.

Of all my contemporaries who did Latin and Greek at school and Oxford, scholar or not, there isn't a single one teaching at a school. One taught for a while at Dulwich College, before switching to Philosophy. He still teaches a little Latin, but in an American college rather than an English school. That's typical. The teaching of even elementary Latin is draining out of schools and into universities, and inevitably that means that standards are dropping. Imagine what the state of mathematics or science would be if nobody started learning it until they were eighteen. Eventually, Latin will be about as well and as widely known as, say, Sanscrit, Aramaic, or ancient Egyptian. Those are other languages that you can learn at university, but not at school.

Cicero had the right words for this desperate situation in the opening line of his attack on Catiline.

"How long will you abuse our patience, Catiline?' he said, in one of the first recorded rhetorical questions. "Oh, the times! Oh, the habits!"

Or, as every schoolboy doesn't know, "*O tempora! O mores!*" If you've read this book properly, however, you can become a 1950s schoolboy all over again and reach the sort of level where you can lean deep into your armchair and bemoan how second-rate everybody else's Latin is.

To get your Latin going, it's worth buying Catullus's and Horace's poems. They're sometimes a bit tricky but, if you buy one of the Loeb translations, they have the English on one side and Latin on the other, and you can work your way through them pretty easily.

Warning: the Loeb translations are a bit dreary and prim – in one translation of a juicy bit of Euripides, "sperm" is translated as "life whiteness".

But, if you can be bothered to keep two books propped open side by side, you couldn't do much better than look at Horace's *Odes* alongside a copy of the recent translation by James Michie, an accomplished poet in English.

To brush up your Latin prose, get the Loeb of Caesar's *Gallic Wars*. Julius Caesar wrote in nice, clear, prep-school Latin.

To read the most famous Roman of them all, perhaps the greatest leader of all time, in his original language and to recite some of the most heart-breaking poetry ever written as it was meant to be read... Is that not reason enough for doing Latin?

THE FINAL LATIN TEST

Here's the bit of Latin I set at the beginning of this book as a test for you to do, the epitaph on Leonardo Bruni's tomb:

> *Postquam Leonardus e vita migravit*
> *Historia luget; eloquentia muta est*
> *Ferturque musas tum Graecas tum*
> *Latinas lacrimas tenere non potuisse.*

I've printed the translation on the opposite page. If you can manage to translate it now, and you know what each verb and noun is doing in the sentence, congratulations – you have the basics. You can now eat as much pistachio ice cream and drink as many proseccos (or, as a Latin Wanker would put it, prosecci) as you want.

If you want to start looking at the Tintorettos, get a weightier book.

Now that Leonardo has died,
History mourns, eloquence is mute
And it is said that both the Greek
And the Latin Muses haven't been able to hold back
                                        their tears.

ACKNOWLEDGMENTS

All at Short Books, especially Vanessa Webb, Aurea Carpenter, Rebecca Nicolson and Emily Fox.

Alex Fox for his drawing.

My parents, Ferdy and Julia Mount, and my brother and sister, William and Mary Mount, for corrections and suggestions.

Dr Adam Beresford of the University of Massachusetts for help *passim*.

Christopher Howse for advice on religious Latin.

Tony Ring, President, the International Wodehouse Association, for the use of Latin by Jeeves and Wooster.

The editor and publisher of *The Spectator* for permission to adapt *Return of the Dark Ages* [April 2004].

The mistakes are all my own.

Harry Mount, Greenwich Village, New York,
August 2006